MOVIE ★ ICONS

HEPBURN

LTD

CONTENTS

1

KATHARINE HEPBURN: MODERN WOMAN

BY ALAIN SILVER

★

KATHARINE HEPBURN: DIE FRAU VON HEUTE

KATHARINE HEPBURN : UNE FEMME MODERNE

KATHARINE HEPBURN: MODERN WOMAN

by Alain Silver

"I suppose when I was a very young actress, I was very unsure of myself. I thought you had to be nice to everybody, so I was. Then I got to be a big star rather quickly, and it occurred to me that you didn't."

Before the word diva crossed over from opera to movies, there was simply 'Hepburn.' For some, Katharine Hepburn was 'the first lady of cinema,' an epithet that was heavily ironic for the hordes of co-workers who endured her wrath. Hepburn seldom tried to sugarcoat her opinions or her demeanor. Accordingly, she was also 'Katharine of Arrogance,' a slightly exaggerated sobriquet for someone who called herself a fool as often as she did others. "I came along at a point in the movie industry when nothing like me had ever existed, with a loud voice and a very definite personality and a rather belligerent look. Show me an actress who isn't a personality," Hepburn proclaimed, "and you'll show me a woman who isn't a star."

In a life that lasted almost a century, Katharine Hepburn seemed destined to represent the modern woman on stage, on screen, and in the world. The namesake of her mother, a pamphleteer for women's suffrage, Hepburn possessed an athleticism and patrician bearing that combined aspects of Babe Didrikson Zaharias and Greta Garbo, both of whom she admired. As fiercely competitive as Didrikson, Hepburn also shared her deep-rooted integrity and a readiness to penalize herself for transgressions. As fiercely private as Garbo, Hepburn eventually disclosed herself to the world through her autobiographical writings. As fiercely independent as any professional woman, she was managed by her surgeon father – who never approved of her career – until his death.

If her talent was prodigious, effectively and easily ranging from screwball comedy to the overweening gloom of Eugene O'Neill, it wasn't merely talent that set her on the road to becoming an icon. From her first movies, Hepburn learned how stage and screen differed and moved past Dorothy Parker's celebrated witticism that 'she runs the gamut of emotions from A

"Write whatever you want about me but never the truth. No, not that."
Katharine Hepburn

PORTRAIT FOR 'SYLVIA SCARLETT' (1935)

to B.' Whether the film was melodramatic or mirthful, it was Hepburn's presence, the 'definite personality,' that ultimately led to four Academy Awards. "You had to look at her, you had to listen to her," noted Cary Grant, "there was no escaping her; but it wasn't just the beauty, it was the style."

Much of that style was androgynous: lanky figure, high cheekbones, penetrating eyes. As a child, Hepburn was a tomboy; as an adult, she reveled in certain 'mannish' preferences. She imbued characters such as Jo in *Little Women* (1933) with these aspects and even masqueraded as a male in *Sylvia Scarlett* (1935). David O. Selznick, who oversaw her early career at RKO, found her unattractive and refused to cast her in *Gone with the Wind* (1939) because she lacked "sex qualities." Parker and Selznick notwithstanding, few women failed to admire Hepburn and few men could resist her charms: before she was 30, she captivated both director John Ford and mogul Howard Hughes. Purported religious considerations or her family's disapproval kept Hepburn from marrying; but for whatever reasons, her lifelong spinsterhood merely enhanced her reputation as an indomitable woman. In *A Woman Rebels* (1936), Hepburn portrayed a Victorian proto-feminist who transforms a woman's magazine by writing about the oppression of her gender. Her character has an affair with a married man who cannot divorce his wife, which ironically anticipates the key aspect of her almost three-decade relationship with Spencer Tracy.

Hepburn championed woman writers and directors, noting that "the reason many women have gone into directing is to be able to control the images of women on screen." While she extensively revised many scripts, she never took writing credit. Her second movie, *Christopher Strong* (1933), was the only time she worked with a woman director: "Dorothy Arzner was very good. She wore pants. So did I." Although such renowned autocrats as Ford and David Lean permitted her to direct scenes in the only pictures they did with her, Hepburn never took on Arzner's job. While 'wearing the pants' could be a literal and figurative prerogative, what most separated Hepburn from contemporary female stars was her fiscal and physical independence from Hollywood. She bought herself out of one studio contract and packaged herself into another. During a stage and screen career that spanned eight decades, her home was never in Hollywood or New York but always Connecticut where she was born and where she died, still more critical of herself than of others: "I could have accomplished three times what I've accomplished. I haven't realized my full potential. It's disgusting."

ENDPAPERS/VORSATZBLATT/PAGE DE GARDE
PORTRAIT

PAGES 2/3
ON THE SET OF 'THE AFRICAN QUEEN' (1951)

PAGE 4
PORTRAIT (1935)

PAGES 6/7
PORTRAIT

PAGE 8
PORTRAIT

OPPOSITE/RECHTS/CI-CONTRE
PORTRAIT

KATHARINE HEPBURN: DIE FRAU VON HEUTE

von Alain Silver

„Als ich noch eine sehr junge Schauspielerin war, hatte ich vermutlich wenig Selbstvertrauen. Ich dachte, man müsse zu allen nett sein, also war ich es auch. Dann wurde ich ziemlich schnell ein großer Star, und da bemerkte ich, man muss es gar nicht."

Bevor der Begriff „Diva" den Sprung von der Oper zum Film schaffte, hieß es schlicht und einfach „Hepburn". Für manche war Katharine Hepburn die „First Lady des Kinos", was für die Scharen ihrer Mitarbeiter, die täglich ihrem Zorn ausgesetzt waren, wie bittere Ironie klang. Hepburn vertrat ihre Ansichten offen und ohne Umschweife, und in ihrem Verhalten war sie ebenso direkt. Dies trug ihr auch den Spitznamen „Katharine von Arroganzien" ein, was leicht übertrieben scheint, wenn man bedenkt, dass sie sich selbst ebenso oft als „dumm" und „närrisch" bezeichnete wie andere auch. „Zu dem Zeitpunkt, an dem ich ins Filmgeschäft einstieg, hatte es jemanden wie mich noch nie gegeben: mit einer lauten Stimme und klar umrissenen Persönlichkeit und einem recht streitsüchtigen Auftreten. Zeigen Sie mir eine Schauspielerin ohne Persönlichkeit", forderte Hepburn, „und ich zeige Ihnen eine Frau, die kein Star ist."

In einem Leben, das fast ein ganzes Jahrhundert währte, schien Katharine Hepburn dazu bestimmt, die Frau von heute zu verkörpern – auf der Bühne, auf der Leinwand und im Leben. Sie trug den gleichen Namen wie ihre Mutter, die einst für das Frauenwahlrecht auf die Straße gegangen war und Flugblätter verteilt hatte. Mutter wie Tochter besaßen die Sportlichkeit einer „Babe" Didrikson Zaharias und das aristokratische Gehabe einer Greta Garbo, die Katharine beide bewunderte. Sie war nicht nur ehrgeizig im Wettkampf wie Didrikson, sondern ebenso integer und jederzeit bereit, sich selbst für Fehltritte zu kasteien. Andererseits kapselte sie sich wie die Garbo ab und offenbarte ihr Innenleben erst allmählich in ihren autobiografischen Schriften. Wie jede berufstätige Frau legte sie großen Wert auf ihre Unabhängigkeit. Ihr Vater – ein Chirurg, der mit ihrer Karriere nie einverstanden war – agierte bis zu seinem Tod als ihr Manager.

Sie wusste mit gleicher Leichtigkeit und Wirksamkeit in einer Screwballkomödie oder in einem der unendlich düsteren Stücke von Eugene O'Neill aufzutreten. Doch nicht nur ihr erstaunliches Talent machte sie zur Ikone. Von ihren ersten Filmen an erkannte Hepburn die Unterschiede

„Schreiben Sie über mich, was Sie wollen, aber niemals die Wahrheit. Nein, nur die nicht."
Katharine Hepburn

PORTRAIT (1935)

zwischen Bühne und Film, und rasch setzte sie sich über Dorothy Parkers berühmtes Bonmot hinweg, sie beherrsche „die gesamte Gefühlsskala von A bis B". Ob ein Film heiter oder melodramatisch war – Hepburns Präsenz und ihre „klar umrissene Persönlichkeit" brachten ihr letztendlich vier Oscars ein. „Man musste sie einfach anschauen, ihr zuhören", meinte Cary Grant. „Man konnte sich ihr nicht entziehen, aber es war nicht bloß die Schönheit, es war ihr Stil."

Und dieser war vor allem androgyn: schlaksige Figur, hohe Wangenknochen, durchdringender Blick. Als Kind war Hepburn eine jungenhafte Range, als Erwachsene pflegte sie gewisse „männliche" Vorlieben. Diese Eigenschaften übertrug sie auf Figuren wie die Jo in *Vier Schwestern* (1933), und in *Sylvia Scarlett* (1935) verkleidete sie sich gar als Mann. David O. Selznick, der über die Anfangsjahre ihrer Karriere bei RKO wachte, fand sie unattraktiv und mochte ihr wegen fehlender „Sexqualitäten" keine Rolle in *Vom Winde verweht* (1939) geben. Trotzdem gab es nur wenige Frauen, die Hepburn nicht bewunderten, und wenige Männer konnten sich ihrem Charme entziehen: Bevor sie 30 wurde, hatte sie den Regisseur John Ford wie auch den Mogul Howard Hughes um den Finger gewickelt. Ob es angebliche religiöse Bedenken oder die Missbilligung durch ihr Elternhaus waren, die Hepburn vom Heiraten abhielten – ihr Leben als „alte Jungfer" unterstrich jedenfalls ihren Ruf als Unbezwingbare. In *Ein aufsässiges Mädchen* (1936) stellt Hepburn eine Protofeministin der viktorianischen Zeit dar, die eine Frauenzeitschrift auf den Kopf stellt, indem sie entgegen aller Gepflogenheit über die Unterdrückung ihres Geschlechts schreibt. Im Film lässt sie sich auf eine Liebesaffäre mit einem verheirateten Mann ein, der sich nicht von seiner Frau scheiden lassen kann, was als ironische Vorwegnahme ihrer fast drei Jahrzehnte währenden Beziehung zu Spencer Tracy erscheint.

Hepburns Engagement für Autorinnen und Regisseurinnen gründete auf der Überzeugung, dass viele Frauen das Regiefach eigens erlernten, weil sie nur so „die Darstellung der Frau auf der Leinwand" steuern konnten. Obschon sie zahlreiche Drehbücher in großem Umfang redigierte, beanspruchte sie nie die Nennung als Mitautorin. Bei ihrem zweiten Film *Christopher Strong* (1933) arbeitete sie das einzige Mal mit einer Regisseurin: „Dorothy Arzner war sehr gut. Sie trug Hosen. Ich auch." Notorische Autokraten wie John Ford und David Lean gestatteten Hepburn in den jeweils einzigen Filmen, die sie mit ihr drehten, bei einzelnen Szenen Regie zu führen, doch sie wechselte nie in dieses Fach. Wenngleich es im wörtlichen wie im übertragenen Sinn Hepburns Vorrecht gewesen sein mag, „Hosen zu tragen", stellt doch ihre finanzielle wie geografische Unabhängigkeit von Hollywood den größten Unterschied zu weiblichen Stars von heute dar. Sie kaufte sich aus einem Studiovertrag frei und machte sich selbst zum Bestandteil eines Pakets, das sie dann an Hollywood verkaufte. Während ihrer Theater- und Filmkarriere, die sich über acht Jahrzehnte erstreckte, wohnte sie niemals in Hollywood oder New York, sondern stets in Connecticut, wo sie geboren wurde und auch starb. Und selbst am Ende stand sie sich selbst noch immer kritischer gegenüber als anderen: „Ich hätte das Dreifache des tatsächlich Erreichten erreichen können. Ich habe mein Potential nicht voll ausgeschöpft. Das kotzt mich an."

ON THE SET OF 'LITTLE WOMEN' (1933)

KATHARINE HEPBURN : UNE FEMME MODERNE

Alain Silver

« Au tout début de ma carrière, je n'étais pas sûre de moi. Je pensais qu'il fallait être aimable avec tout le monde. Et puis je suis assez rapidement devenue une star, et j'ai réalisé que ce n'était pas la peine. »

Avant que le mot « diva » ne passe du monde de l'opéra à celui du cinéma, on disait simplement « Hepburn ». Pour certains, Katharine Hepburn est « la première dame du cinéma », épithète un brin ironique aux yeux des hordes de collaborateurs contraints d'endurer son courroux. Hepburn se donne rarement la peine d'enrober ses propos. Par conséquent, on la surnomme également « Katharine de l'Arrogance », sobriquet somme toute excessif pour une femme qui se montre aussi dure envers elle-même qu'envers les autres. « J'ai débarqué dans l'industrie du cinéma à une époque où on n'avait jamais rien vu de tel, une femme avec une voix tonitruante, une personnalité très affirmée et une allure belliqueuse », explique-t-elle. « Trouvez-moi une actrice qui n'ait pas une forte personnalité et vous verrez si c'est une star. »

En près d'un siècle d'existence, Katharine Hepburn semblait prédestinée à incarner la femme moderne, aussi bien à la ville que sur les planches et à l'écran. De sa mère, suffragette militante dont elle a hérité du prénom, Hepburn tient une silhouette athlétique et un port aristocratique rappelant à la fois l'athlète Babe Didrikson Zaharias et l'actrice Greta Garbo, deux femmes qu'elle admire. Dotée d'un esprit de compétition aussi féroce que Didrikson, Hepburn possède également la même intégrité et la même volonté de se punir de ses fautes. Défendant aussi jalousement sa vie privée que Garbo, elle finira par se révéler au grand jour par le biais de ses écrits autobiographiques. Aussi farouchement indépendante qu'une femme d'affaires, elle est managée par son père – qui n'approuvera jamais sa carrière – jusqu'à la mort de ce dernier.

Si son prodigieux talent lui permet de passer sans effort de la comédie loufoque au pessimisme outré d'Eugene O'Neill, ce n'est pas grâce à son seul talent qu'elle prend le chemin de la gloire. Dès ses premiers films, Hepburn comprend la différence entre le théâtre et le cinéma et passe outre la célèbre raillerie de Dorothy Parker, qui déclare qu'« elle décline toute la

STILL FROM 'ADAM'S RIB' (1949)

« Écrivez ce que vous voulez sur moi, mais jamais la vérité. Non, pas ça. »
Katharine Hepburn

gamme des émotions de A à B». Que le film soit mélodramatique ou joyeux, c'est grâce à sa présence, à sa «personnalité affirmée», que Katharine Hepburn obtient en fin de compte ses quatre oscars. «On était obligé de la regarder, de l'écouter», note Cary Grant, «il était impossible de lui échapper. Mais ce n'était pas seulement à cause de sa beauté, c'était aussi à cause de son style.»

Un style pour le moins androgyne avec sa silhouette dégingandée, ses pommettes saillantes et son regard pénétrant. Enfant, Hepburn est un garçon manqué; adulte, elle se complaît dans ses préférences «masculines». Elle en imprègne certains personnages tels que Jo dans *Les Quatre Filles du docteur March* (1933) et se déguise même en homme dans *Sylvia Scarlett* (1935). David O. Selznick, qui supervise ses débuts chez RKO, la trouve peu séduisante et refuse de la faire jouer dans *Autant en emporte le vent* (1939), lui reprochant de manquer de sex-appeal. N'en déplaise à Dorothy Parker et à David Selznick, rares sont pourtant les femmes dont elle ne suscite pas l'admiration et les hommes qui résistent à son charme: avant l'âge de 30 ans, elle a charmé le cinéaste John Ford et le milliardaire Howard Hughes. Mais après l'échec de son premier mariage, elle ne se remariera jamais. Que son célibat soit dû à des considérations religieuses ou à la désapprobation de sa famille, il ne fait que renforcer sa réputation de femme indomptable. Dans *La Rebelle* (1936), elle incarne une proto-féministe victorienne qui transforme un magazine féminin en dénonçant l'oppression de ses semblables. Son personnage a une liaison avec un homme marié qui ne peut divorcer de sa femme, ce qui préfigure étrangement la relation que l'actrice aura pendant vingt-sept ans avec Spencer Tracy.

Katharine Hepburn soutient ses consœurs scénaristes et réalisatrices, soulignant que «si elles se sont lancées dans le cinéma, c'est pour pouvoir changer l'image de la femme à l'écran». Bien qu'elle révise de nombreux scénarios, sa contribution ne figure jamais au générique. Son deuxième film, *Le Phalène d'argent* (1933), marque sa seule collaboration avec une réalisatrice: «Dorothy Arzner était excellente. Elle portait des pantalons. Moi aussi.» Bien que des autocrates réputés tels que John Ford et David Lean la laissent tourner des scènes dans les seuls films qu'ils réalisent avec elle, Hepburn ne passera jamais derrière la caméra. Même si «porter la culotte» est l'une de ses prérogatives au sens propre comme au figuré, ce qui la distingue le plus des autres vedettes féminines de l'époque est son indépendance financière à l'égard de Hollywood. Après avoir racheté son premier contrat, elle pose ses conditions avant d'en accepter un autre. Au cours d'une carrière théâtrale et cinématographique à cheval sur huit décennies, elle n'habitera jamais New York ni Hollywood, mais restera dans le Connecticut qui l'a vue naître et qui la verra mourir. Jusqu'à la fin, elle se montrera toujours plus critique envers elle-même qu'envers les autres: «J'aurais pu accomplir trois fois ce que j'ai accompli. Je n'ai pas pleinement réalisé mon potentiel. C'est révoltant.»

PAGE 22
BRYN MAWR (1928)
Hepburn's first appearance on stage (in Baltimore). / Hepburn steht erstmals auf der Bühne (in Baltimore). / Sa première apparition sur scène (à Baltimore).

ON THE SET OF 'UNDERCURRENT' (1946)

2

VISUAL FILMOGRAPHY

FILMOGRAFIE IN BILDERN
FILMOGRAPHIE EN IMAGES

EARLY DAYS

★

DIE FRÜHEN JAHRE

LES DÉBUTS

"Acting is a business you go into because you're an egocentric. It's a very embarrassing profession."
Katharine Hepburn

„Die Schauspielerei ist ein Geschäft für Egozentriker. Es ist ein sehr peinlicher Beruf."
Katharine Hepburn

« Le métier d'acteur est une profession que l'on choisit par égocentrisme. C'est très embarrassant. »
Katharine Hepburn

STAGE PRODUCTION 'THE WARRIOR'S HUSBAND' (1932)
A first appearance on Broadway: setting the tone for mannish roles. / Erster Auftritt am Broadway: Auftakt zu vielen jungenhaften Rollen. / Sa première apparition à Broadway donne le ton de ses rôles de garçon manqué.

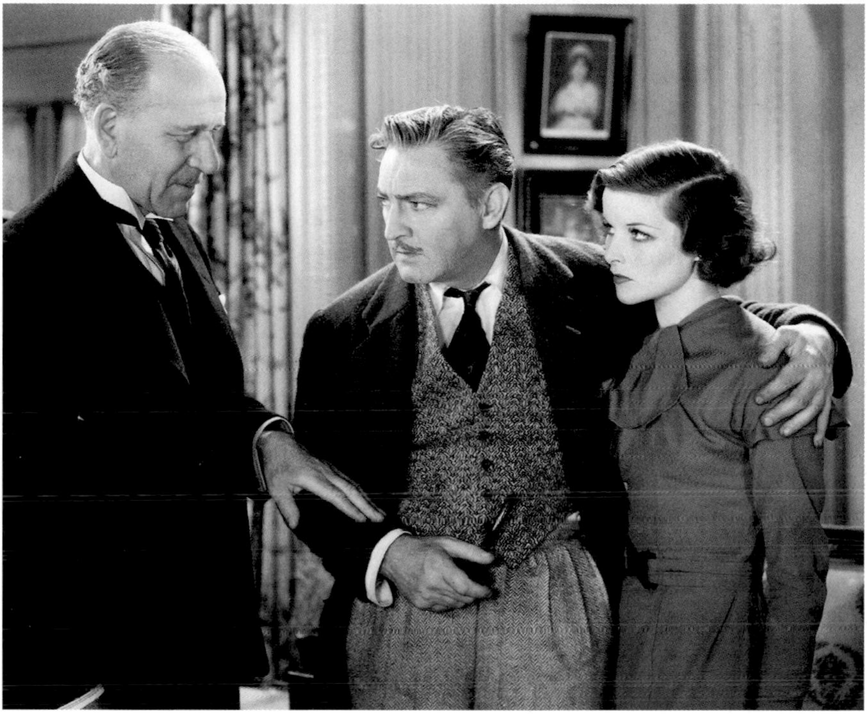

STILL FROM 'A BILL OF DIVORCEMENT' (1932)
With the legendary John Barrymore (center). / Mit dem legendären John Barrymore (Mitte). / Aux côtés du légendaire John Barrymore (au centre).

STILL FROM 'A BILL OF DIVORCEMENT' (1932)
Her first feature: posed with 'soft' love interest David Manners. / Ihr erster Spielfilm: Hier posiert sie als Sydney mit ihrem „Softie"-Liebhaber (David Manners). / Dans son premier film, posant sagement avec son prétendant (David Manners).

ON THE SET OF 'CHRISTOPHER STRONG' (1933)
Another proto-feminist portrayal in her second feature. / Eine weitere protofeministische Rolle in ihrem zweiten Spielfilm. / Autre rôle proto-féministe pour son deuxième film.

PAGES 30/31
STILL FROM 'CHRISTOPHER STRONG' (1933)
In a more feminine moment with Colin Clive (the title character). / In einer weiblicheren Pose mit Colin Clive, der die Titelrolle spielt. / Une attitude plus féminine dans les bras du héros (Colin Clive).

PORTRAIT FOR 'CHRISTOPHER STRONG' (1933)
Hepburn's character was loosely inspired by Amelia Earhart. / Hepburns Rolle wurde in groben Zügen von der Fliegerin Amelia Earhart inspiriert. / Son personnage s'inspire librement de l'aviatrice Amelia Earhart.

STILL FROM 'MORNING GLORY' (1933)
Only her third feature but already traces of autobiography and an Oscar nomination. / Ihr dritter Film trägt bereits autobiographische Züge und bringt ihr eine Oscar-Nominierung ein. / Un troisième film aux accents déjà autobiographiques, qui lui vaut son premier oscar.

"I don't really care about the Oscars, but wouldn't you know it: I have more of the damn things than anybody."
Katharine Hepburn

„Die ‚Oscars' sind mir eigentlich ziemlich egal, aber zufällig hab ich mehr von den verdammten Dingern als sonst jemand."
Katharine Hepburn

« Je ne me soucie guère des oscars, et figurez-vous que c'est moi qui ai reçu le plus de ces satanés machins. »
Katharine Hepburn

STILL FROM 'MORNING GLORY' (1933)
With Douglas Fairbanks Jr. in a play within a movie. / Mit Douglas Fairbanks Jr. tritt sie im Film in einem Theaterstück auf. / Pièce de théâtre à l'intérieur du film, aux côtés de Douglas Fairbanks Jr.

PAGES 34/35
ADVERT FOR 'MORNING GLORY' (1933)

An Example

of what RKO RADIO means by its promise of finer shows than ever this season.

The greatest of stars, fine supporting casts in notable plays by distinguished authors, produced by the outstanding directors of screen art.

That is our pledge and here is our proof!

"MORNING GLORY"

KATHARINE HEPBURN

DOUGLAS FAIRBANKS, JR.

ADOLPHE MENJOU

MARY DUNCAN · C. AUBREY SMITH

From the play by

ZOE AKINS

DIRECTED BY

LOWELL SHERMAN

THE HUMAN
and real story of the small town girl who "just knew" that Broadway couldn't get along without her. With oceans of faith and an empty purse she went
down
the
scale
—until a great love found her.

STILL FROM 'LITTLE WOMEN' (1933)
RKO's homespun visualization of Alcott's family of women. / Louisa May Alcotts Frauenwirtschaft in der schlichten Version von RKO. / L'adaptation des *Quatre Filles du docteur March* par la RKO.

PORTRAIT FOR 'LITTLE WOMEN' (1933)
A wistful moment as 'Jo.' / Ein wehmütiger Augenblick für Jo. / Moment de mélancolie pour Jo March.

STILL FROM 'LITTLE WOMEN' (1933)
Another play within a movie, an early motif of Hepburn features. / Und noch ein Theaterstück im Film – ein frühes Motiv der Hepburn-Filme. / Autre pièce de théâtre à l'intérieur du film, thème récurrent à ses débuts.

"I was totally unaware
that we were the second-rate sex."
Katharine Hepburn

„Ich hatte überhaupt keine Ahnung davon,
dass wir das Geschlecht zweiter Klasse waren."
Katharine Hepburn

« J'ignorais totalement
que nous étions un sexe de seconde zone. »
Katharine Hepburn

STILL FROM 'LITTLE WOMEN' (1933)
Hepburn transformed 'Jo' into an innocent sophisticate. / Hepburn stellte Jo als ebenso unschuldig wie raffiniert dar. / Hepburn transforme Jo en une élégante innocente.

STILL FROM 'LITTLE WOMEN' (1933)
Hepburn often injects a tomboy aspect into romantic moments. / In romantische Szenen lässt Hepburn immer wieder etwas Jungenhaftes einfließen. / Hepburn apporte souvent un côté « garçon manqué » aux scènes romantiques.

PAGES 42/43
ADVERT FOR 'LITTLE WOMEN' (1933)

ON THE SET OF 'LITTLE WOMEN' (1933)
With George Cukor, who directed her in ten projects. / Mit George Cukor, unter dessen Regie sie in zehn Filmen spielte. / Aux côtés de George Cukor, avec lequel elle tournera dix films.

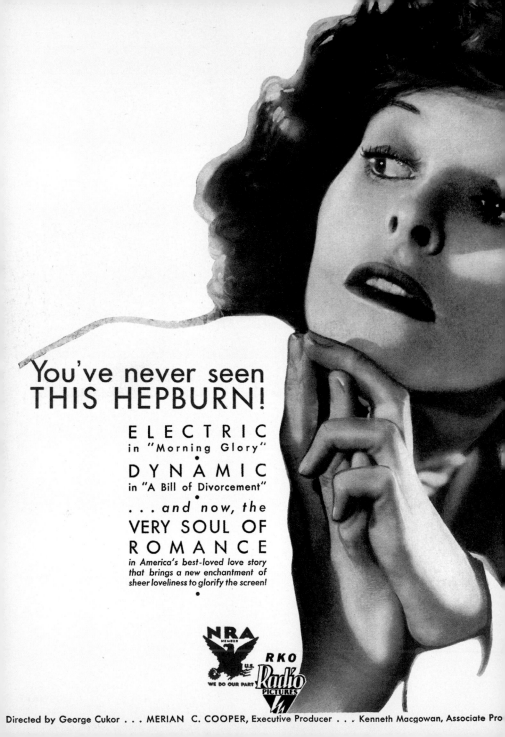

You've never seen THIS HEPBURN!

ELECTRIC
in "Morning Glory"

•

DYNAMIC
in "A Bill of Divorcement"

•

. . . *and now, the*

VERY SOUL OF ROMANCE

in America's best-loved love story that brings a new enchantment of sheer loveliness to glorify the screen!

•

NRA MEMBER U.S. WE DO OUR PART

RKO Radio PICTURES

Directed by George Cukor . . . MERIAN C. COOPER, Executive Producer . . . Kenneth Macgowan, Associate Pro

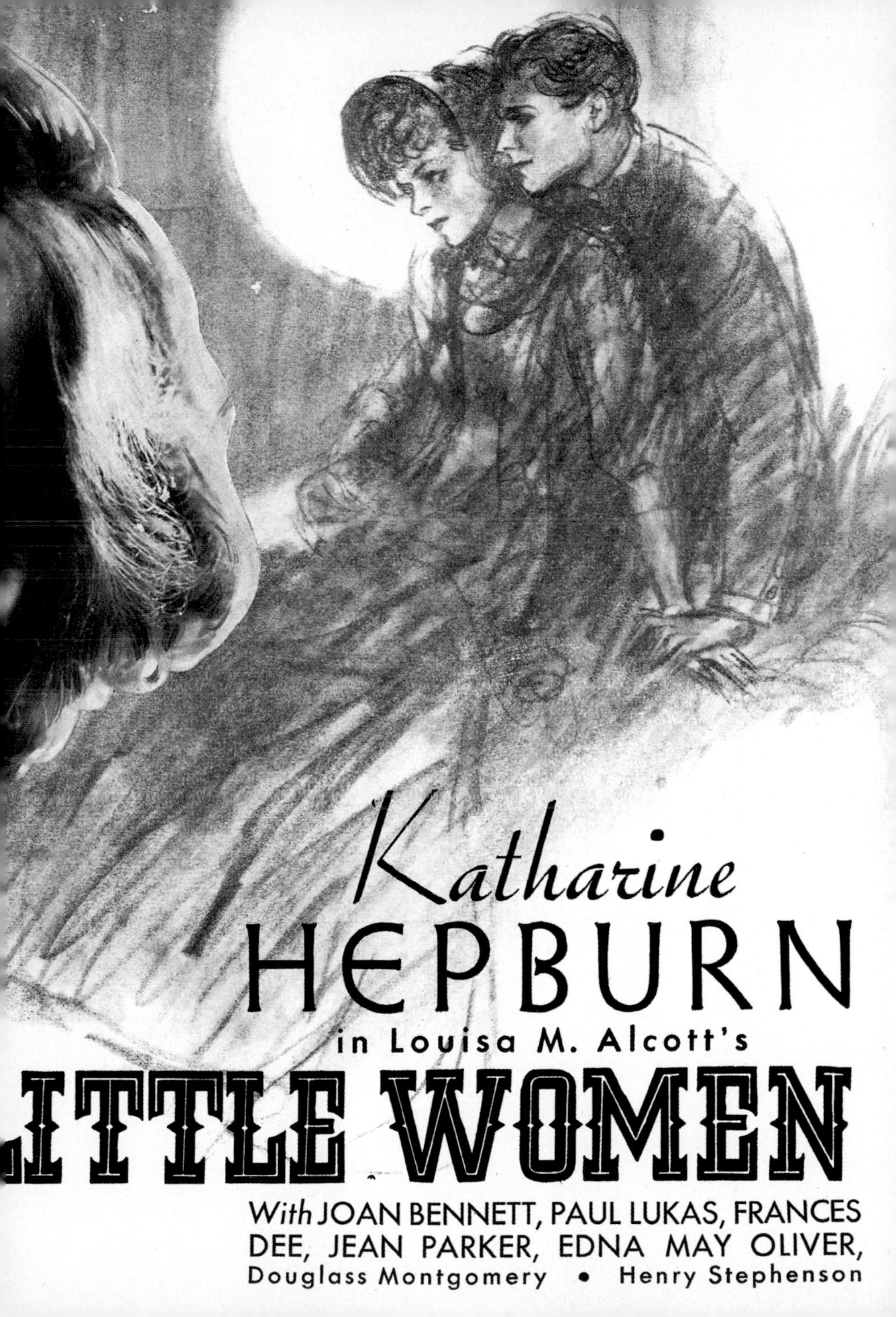
Katharine
HEPBURN
in Louisa M. Alcott's
ITTLE WOMEN
With JOAN BENNETT, PAUL LUKAS, FRANCES DEE, JEAN PARKER, EDNA MAY OLIVER,
Douglass Montgomery • Henry Stephenson

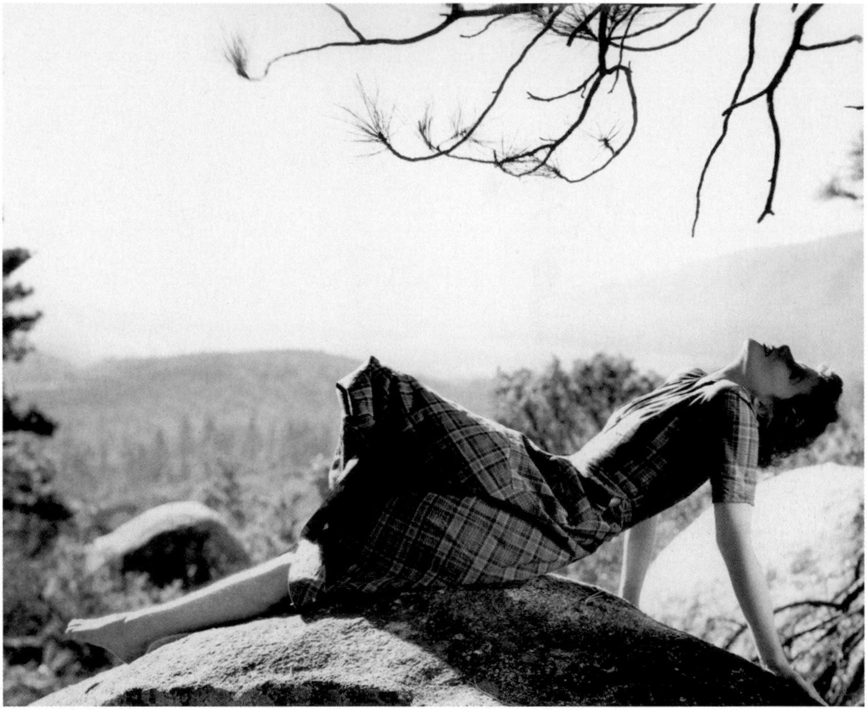

STILL FROM 'SPITFIRE' (1934)
Hepburn bizarrely cast as a semiliterate mountain girl. / Hepburn wirkt in der Rolle eines halbgebildeten Mädchens aus den Bergen leicht fehlbesetzt. / Quelque peu à contre-emploi dans un rôle de montagnarde presque illettrée.

STILL FROM 'SPITFIRE' (1934)
With a caddish Robert Young: "The more I love 'em, the less I trust 'em." / Mit Robert Young in der Schurkenrolle: „Je mehr ich Sie liebe, desto weniger traue ich Ihnen." / Avec le mufle Robert Young : « Plus je les aime, moins je leur fais confiance. »

"Acting is the most minor of gifts. Never forget that they don't give a Nobel Prize for it, and that Shirley Temple was doing it perfectly adequately at the age of four."
Katharine Hepburn

„Schauspielen ist die allergeringste Begabung. Vergessen Sie nicht, dass es dafür keinen Nobelpreis gibt und Shirley Temple es schon im Alter von vier Jahren hinlänglich beherrschte."
Katharine Hepburn

« Le talent d'acteur est un don extrêmement mineur. N'oubliez pas qu'on ne lui décerne pas de prix Nobel et que Shirley Temple le possédait parfaitement à l'âge de quatre ans. »
Katharine Hepburn

STAGE PRODUCTION 'THE LAKE' (1933)
An immediate return to stagebound elegance, which Dorothy Parker mocked. / Sofort kehrt sie zur Eleganz des Theaters zurück, über die sich Dorothy Parker lustig machte. / Un retour au théâtre qui lui vaudra les railleries de Dorothy Parker.

SCREEN TEST 'JOAN OF ARC' (1934)
From earthy hillbilly to saintly mystic, no role was impossible for the young Hepburn. / Vom derben Landei zur verklärten Mystikerin – keine Rolle schien die junge Hepburn zu überfordern. / De la paysanne à la mystique, aucun rôle n'est hors de sa portée.

ADVERT FOR 'LONG LOST FATHER' (1934)
A planned reteaming with Barrymore that never happened. / Es kam nicht zu der erneuten Zusammenarbeit mit Barrymore vor der Kamera. / Un nouveau projet avec John Barrymore qui ne verra jamais le jour.

BARRYMORE . . HEPBURN

"LONG LOST FATHER"

★ ★

The brilliant personalities of "A Bill of Divorcement"

TOGETHER AGAIN!

From the new international best selling novel by G. B. Stern.

The story of a devil-may-care father and a go-to-the-devil daughter who met for the first time on the downward path.

MAGNETIC!

Realize the power of this double draw! A co-starring combination seldom equalled in the history of shows!

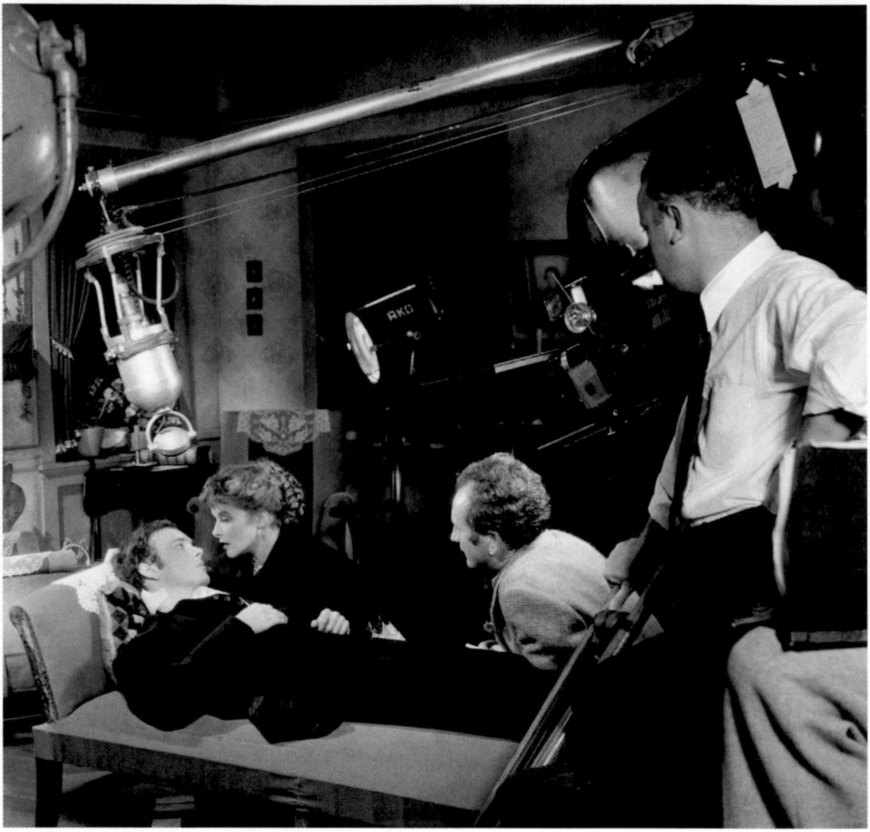

ON THE SET OF 'THE LITTLE MINISTER' (1934)
Director Richard Wallace watches an intimate moment between John Beal and Katharine Hepburn. / Regisseur Richard Wallace beobachtet einen Augenblick der Intimität zwischen John Beal und Katharine Hepburn. / Le réalisateur Richard Wallace observe John Beal et Katharine Hepburn pendant le tournage d'une scène d'intimité.

PAGES 51–57
ADVERT FOR 'THE LITTLE MINISTER' (1934)
Even in a period dress, Hepburn's gypsy girl character can run like a boy. / Selbst im historischen Kostüm kann das von Hepburn gespielte Zigeunermädchen wie ein Junge rennen. / Même en robe de gitane, Hepburn est capable de courir comme un garçon.

R

N

STILL FROM 'BREAK OF HEARTS' (1935)
With her philandering husband, portrayed by Charles Boyer. / Mit Charles Boyer in der Rolle eines Ehemanns, der ein notorischer Schürzenjäger ist. / Avec son mari coureur de jupons (Charles Boyer).

PAGES 60/61
STILL FROM 'ALICE ADAMS' (1935)
Hepburn walked through this portrayal into another Oscar nomination. / Diese Rolle brachte Hepburn eine weitere Oscar-Nominierung ein. / Son interprétation dans *Désirs secrets* lui vaut une deuxième sélection aux Oscars.

PORTRAIT FOR 'BREAK OF HEARTS' (1935)
Dressed 'creatively' as an aspiring composer who marries a conductor. / „Kreativ" gekleidet als aufstrebende Komponistin, die einen Dirigenten heiratet. / Tenue extravagante pour Constance, compositrice en herbe mariée à un chef d'orchestre.

STILL FROM 'SYLVIA SCARLETT' (1935)
The first of four features with Cary Grant. / Der erste von vier Spielfilmen mit Cary Grant. / Le premier de quatre films avec Cary Grant.

"If you always do what interests you, at least one person is pleased."
Katharine Hepburn

„Wenn du immer das tust, was dich interessiert, dann freut sich wenigstens einer."
Katharine Hepburn

« Si vous faites toujours ce qui vous plaît, il y aura au moins une personne qui sera contente. »
Katharine Hepburn

STILL FROM 'SYLVIA SCARLETT' (1935)
The plot required Hepburn's character to masquerade as a man. / Die Handlung verlangte, dass Hepburn sich als Mann verkleidet. / L'héroïne qu'elle incarne est obligée de se déguiser en homme.

PAGES 64/65
PORTRAIT FOR 'SYLVIA SCARLETT' (1935)
Director George Cukor used the opportunity to emphasize Hepburn's boyish beauty. / Regisseur George Cukor nutzte die Gelegenheit, um Hepburns jungenhafte Schönheit hervorzuheben. / Le réalisateur George Cukor en profite pour souligner sa beauté masculine.

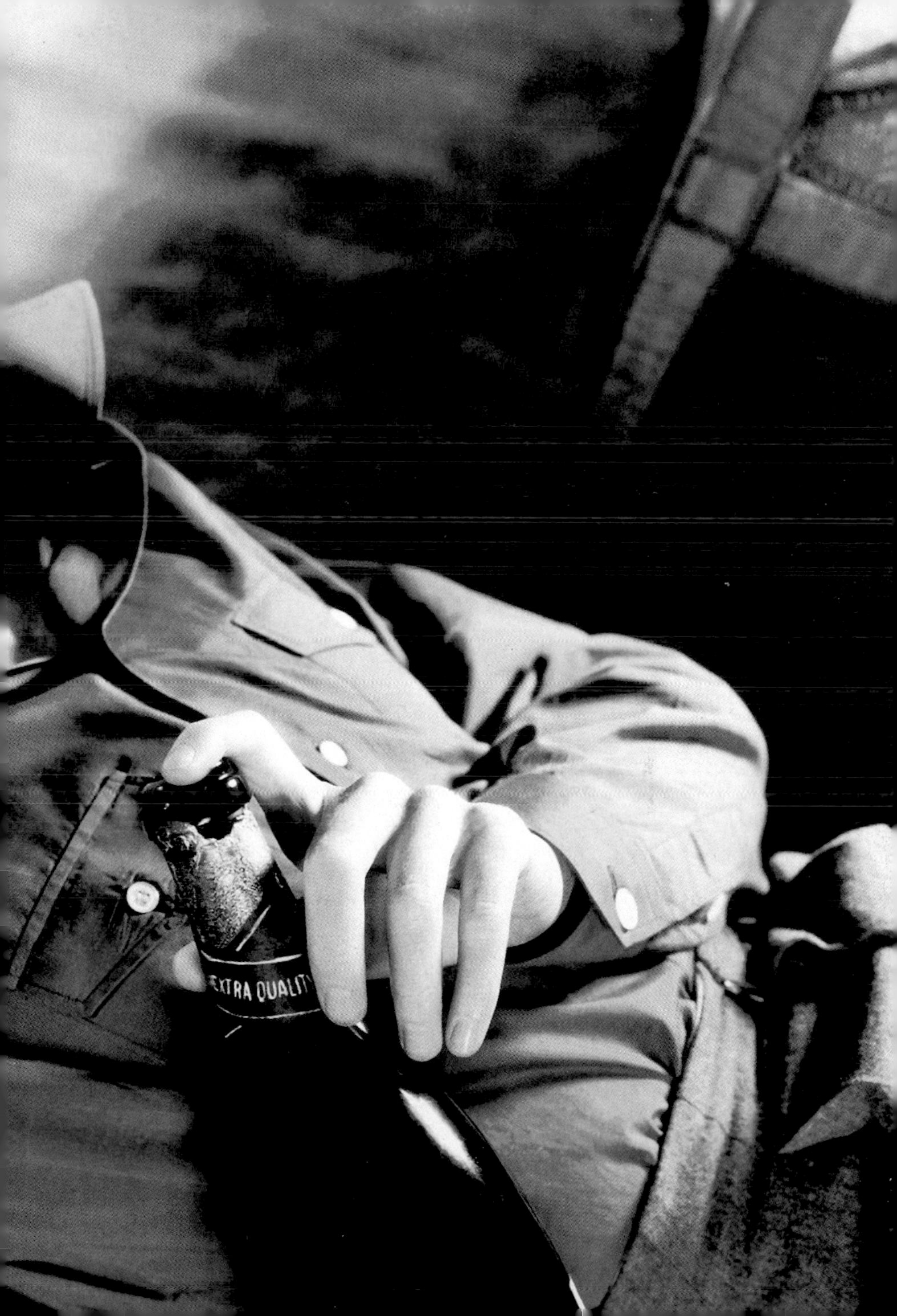
EXTRA QUALITY

"Plain women know more about men than beautiful women do. But beautiful women don't need to know about men. It's the men who have to know about beautiful women."
Katharine Hepburn

„Unattraktive Frauen wissen mehr über Männer als schöne Frauen. Aber schöne Frauen müssen nichts über Männer wissen. Die Männer müssen Bescheid wissen über schöne Frauen."
Katharine Hepburn

« Les femmes quelconques connaissent mieux les hommes que les belles femmes. Mais les belles femmes n'ont pas besoin de connaître les hommes. Ce sont les hommes qui doivent connaître les belles femmes. »
Katharine Hepburn

PAGES 68/69
PORTRAIT FOR 'MARY OF SCOTLAND' (1936)
Hepburn's hauteur swept a usually indomitable director, John Ford, off his feet. / Vor Hepburns Arroganz ging sogar ein so willensstarker Regisseur wie John Ford in die Knie. / Son tempérament hautain a raison du caractère réputé indomptable du réalisateur John Ford.

PORTRAIT FOR 'SYLVIA SCARLETT' (1935)

STILL FROM 'A WOMAN REBELS' (1936)
As an explicit feminist in Victorian England fearing neither man nor beast. / Als erklärte Feministin im viktorianischen England fürchtet sie weder Männer noch Tiere. / Un personnage intrépide et ouvertement féministe dans l'Angleterre victorienne.

PORTRAIT FOR 'A WOMAN REBELS' (1936)
A publicity picture captures a character dynamic: Hepburn looms over Herbert Marshall. / Das Werbefoto bringt die Konstellation der Charaktere auf den Punkt: Hepburn überragt Herbert Marshall. / Une photo publicitaire qui en dit long sur son personnage, toisant dédaigneusement Herbert Marshall.

STILL FROM 'QUALITY STREET' (1937)
Hepburn reteamed with the meticulous director George Stevens for another uninspired period tale from J. M. Barrie aping Jane Austen. / Hepburn arbeitete in dem einfallslosen Kostümstreifen erneut mit dem gewissenhaften Regisseur George Stevens zusammen. Zugrunde lag eine Erzählung von J. M. Barrie in Jane-Austen-Manier. / Retrouvailles avec le réalisateur George Stevens pour un film d'époque peu inspiré d'après une parodie de Jane Austen signée J. M. Barrie.

"You're a hell of a fine girl. If you'd just learn to shut up and knuckle under, you'd probably make somebody a nice wife."
John Ford, director

„Du bist ein verflucht ordentliches Mädchen. Wenn du nur lernen würdest, den Mund zu halten und dich zu fügen, dann wärst du wahrscheinlich für jemanden eine nette Ehefrau."
John Ford, Regisseur

« Tu es une fille épatante. Si tu apprenais seulement à la fermer et à céder de temps en temps, tu ferais sans doute une bonne épouse. »
John Ford, cinéaste

ON THE SET OF 'QUALITY STREET' (1937)

STILL FROM 'STAGE DOOR' (1937)
With Ginger Rogers. / Mit Ginger Rogers. / Aux côtés de Ginger Rogers.

"It would be a terrific innovation if you could get your mind to stretch a little further than the next wisecrack."
Terry Randall, 'Stage Door' (1937)

„Das wäre mal was ganz Neues, wenn du dein Gehirn ein bisschen weiter arbeiten lassen würdest als bis zum nächsten dummen Spruch."
Terry Randall, *Bühneneingang* (1937)

« Ce serait une formidable innovation si tu parvenais à réfléchir un peu plus loin que la prochaine vanne. »
Terry Randall, *Pension d'artistes* (1937)

STILL FROM 'STAGE DOOR' (1937)
Once again Hepburn is an actress portraying an actress. / Wieder einmal spielt Hepburn eine Schauspielerin. / Hepburn incarne une fois de plus une actrice.

STILL FROM 'BRINGING UP BABY' (1938)
This is 30 feet closer than Cary Grant was prepared to act with the 'cat'. / Hier kommt sie der „Katze" um neun Meter näher, als Cary Grant es während der Dreharbeiten wagte. / Beaucoup plus à l'aise avec le « matou » que Cary Grant, qui ne s'en approche pas à moins de dix mètres.

STILL FROM 'BRINGING UP BABY' (1938)
Reteamed with Cary Grant for Howard Hawks' screwball classic. / In Howard Hawks Screwball-Klassiker spielt sie erneut mit Cary Grant. / Retrouvailles avec Cary Grant dans une comédie délirante de Howard Hawks.

STILL FROM 'HOLIDAY' (1938)
Although these films are now classics, at the time they bombed and Hepburn was labeled 'Box Office Poison.' / Obwohl die Filme heute als Klassiker gelten, floppten sie zu ihrer Zeit, und Hepburn galt als „Kassengift". / Ces films devenus des classiques firent un bide à l'époque, valant à Hepburn d'être qualifiée de « poison du box-office ».

PAGE 80
PORTRAIT FOR 'THE PHILADELPHIA STORY' (1940)

STILL FROM 'HOLIDAY' (1938)
Grant is marrying Hepburn's sister, but finds his attitude to life resonates with Hepburn's. / Johnny (Grant) findet in seiner Lebenshaltung größere Übereinstimmung mit Linda (Hepburn), soll aber ihre Schwester heiraten. / Même s'il épouse sa sœur, c'est avec elle que Cary Grant se sent le plus en phase.

INDEPENDENT WOMAN

★

EINE EIGENSTÄNDIGE FRAU

UNE FEMME INDÉPENDANTE

STILL FROM 'THE PHILADELPHIA STORY' (1940)

Hepburn again combined glamour and pratfalls and got another Oscar nod. / Wieder einmal bringt Hepburn Glamour und Slapstick unter einen Hut und verdient sich damit eine weitere Oscar-Nominierung. / Un mélange de glamour et de farce qui lui vaut une nouvelle sélection aux Oscars.

"I don't want to be worshipped. I want to be loved."
Tracy Samantha Lord, 'The Philadelphia Story' (1940)

„Ich möchte nicht angebetet werden. Ich möchte geliebt werden."
Tracy Samantha Lord, *Die Nacht vor der Hochzeit* (1940)

« Je ne veux pas être idolâtrée. Je veux être aimée. »
Tracy Samantha Lord, *Indiscrétions* (1940)

STILL FROM 'THE PHILADELPHIA STORY' (1940)

After two years away, Hepburn returned to films, here opposite the homespun James Stewart. / Nach zwei Jahren Pause kehrt sie auf die Leinwand zurück – an der Seite des schlichten James Stewart. / Retour au cinéma après deux ans d'absence, aux côtés de l'humble James Stewart.

STILL FROM 'THE PHILADELPHIA STORY' (1940)
Hepburn developed the original stage play, made it a success, and Howard Hughes bought the film rights for her. When Hollywood came knocking she was in control. / Hepburn arbeitete am zugrunde liegenden Bühnenstück mit, brachte es zum Erfolg und Howard Hughes erwarb für sie die Filmrechte. Als Hollywood bei ihr anklopfte, hielt sie alle Zügel in der Hand. / Grâce au succès remporté au théâtre et aux droits que Howard Hughes a rachetés pour elle, Hepburn a toutes les cartes en mains lorsque Hollywood décide d'adapter la pièce.

PAGES 86/87
STILL FROM 'WOMAN OF THE YEAR' (1942)
First time on screen with 'soulmate' Spencer Tracy. / Erstmals steht sie neben ihrem „Seelenverwandten" Spencer Tracy vor der Kamera. / Première coopération à l'écran avec son « âme sœur », Spencer Tracy.

STILL FROM 'THE PHILADELPHIA STORY' (1940)

STILL FROM 'WOMAN OF THE YEAR' (1942)
The bride's explicit feminism will threaten their marriage. / Mit ihrem unverblümten Feminismus bringt die Braut die Hochzeit in Gefahr. / Le féminisme affiché de la mariée menacera leur union.

PAGES 90/91
ON THE SET OF 'KEEPER OF THE FLAME' (1942)
This Hepburn/Tracy/Cukor project is a dark morality play. / Bei diesem Hepburn-Tracy-Cukor-Film handelt es sich um ein düsteres Sittengemälde. / Un sombre conte moral qui réunit Hepburn, Tracy et Cukor.

STILL FROM 'WOMAN OF THE YEAR' (1942)
Hepburn's portrayal of a powerful and sexy woman earned her a fourth Oscar nomination. / Hepburns Darstellung einer mächtigen und erotischen Frau brachte ihr die vierte Oscar-Nominierung ein. / Elle campe une femme forte et sexy qui lui vaut une quatrième sélection aux Oscars.

STILL FROM 'DRAGON SEED' (1944)
Playing an Asian woman in what was Hepburn's first war movie. / In ihrem erstem Kriegsfilm spielt Hepburn eine Asiatin. / Hepburn incarne une asiatique dans son premier film de guerre.

STILL FROM 'DRAGON SEED' (1944)
In make-up as Jade Tan, a patrician peasant. / In ihrer Maske als mutige Bäuerin Jade Tan. / Maquillée en Jade Tan, une noble paysanne.

STILL FROM 'WITHOUT LOVE' (1945)
The collaborative tone is again light and romantic. / Die Zusammenarbeit gestaltet sich wieder einmal locker-romantisch. / Une nouvelle collaboration sur un ton léger et romantique.

PAGES 96/97
STILL FROM 'UNDERCURRENT' (1946)
Hepburn's only film noir, here with icon of that genre Robert Mitchum. / Hepburns einziger *Film noir* – hier mit Robert Mitchum, Ikone dieser Gattung. / Son seul film noir, ici aux côtés du symbole du genre, Robert Mitchum.

PORTRAIT FOR 'WITHOUT LOVE' (1945)
Hepburn as a war widow entering into a marriage of convenience. / Hepburn lässt sich als Kriegerwitwe auf eine Zweckheirat ein. / En veuve de guerre contrainte à un mariage de raison.

ON THE SET OF 'UNDERCURRENT' (1946)
Robert Taylor mimics Hepburn's towel-wearing habit. / Robert Taylor äfft Hepburns Marotte nach, mit einem Handtuch auf dem Kopf umherzulaufen. / Robert Taylor se moque de ses habitudes vestimentaires.

PAGES 100/101
STILL FROM 'THE SEA OF GRASS' (1947)
Hepburn is a reluctant frontier woman. / Hepburn spielt eine Frau, die ihrem Mann widerwillig in den Westen gefolgt ist. / En épouse malheureuse pendant la conquête de l'Ouest.

ON THE SET OF 'UNDERCURRENT' (1946)
Hepburn waits for Robert Taylor's close-up as the crew measure the focal length. / Hepburn wartet auf eine Nahaufnahme von Robert Taylor, während die Kameramannschaft die Brennweite bestimmt. / Hepburn attend le gros plan de Robert Taylor tandis que les techniciens mesurent la distance focale.

ON THE SET OF 'THE SEA OF GRASS' (1947)
Director Elia Kazan having fun with Hepburn's footwear. / Regisseur Elia Kazan findet Gefallen an Hepburns Schuhen. / Le metteur en scène Elia Kazan s'amuse avec ses chaussures.

"Sometimes I wonder if men and women really suit each other. Perhaps they should live next door and just visit now and then."
Katharine Hepburn

„Ich frage mich manchmal, ob Männer und Frauen wirklich zueinander passen. Vielleicht sollten sie nur nebenan wohnen und sich ab und zu besuchen."
Katharine Hepburn

« Parfois, je me demande si les hommes et les femmes sont vraiment faits pour vivre ensemble. Ils devraient peut-être rester voisins et se rendre visite de temps à autre. »
Katharine Hepburn

STILL FROM 'THE SEA OF GRASS' (1947)
Hepburn and Tracy in their only period picture together. / Hepburn und Tracy in ihrem einzigen gemeinsamen Film, der nicht in der Gegenwart angesiedelt ist. / Hepburn et Tracy dans leur seul film d'époque.

STILL FROM 'SONG OF LOVE' (1947)
A decidedly unfeminist pose as the supportive wife of a famous composer. / Eine ausgesprochen unfeministische Pose: Die Ehefrau des berühmten Komponisten steht ihrem Mann hilfreich zur Seite. / Pose résolument peu féministe en épouse dévouée d'un célèbre compositeur.

"I don't believe in marriage. It's bloody impractical to love, honor and obey. If it weren't, you wouldn't have to sign a contract."
Katharine Hepburn

„Ich glaube nicht an die Ehe. Es ist verdammt unrealistisch, dass man liebt, ehrt und gehorcht. Andernfalls müsste man ja keinen Vertrag unterschreiben."
Katharine Hepburn

« Je ne crois pas au mariage. Ce n'est vraiment pas pratique d'aimer, d'honorer et d'obéir. Si ça l'était, on ne serait pas obligé de signer un contrat. »
Katharine Hepburn

STILL FROM 'SONG OF LOVE' (1947)
With Paul Henreid as Robert Schumann. / Mit Paul Henreid als Robert Schumann. / Avec Paul Henreid dans le rôle de Robert Schumann.

ON THE SET OF 'SONG OF LOVE' (1947)
Out of period costume, Hepburn relaxes on an orchestra set. / Hepburn entspannt ohne Kostüm in Orchesternähe. / Hepburn se repose en tenue de ville au milieu de l'orchestre.

"No woman could ever run for president. She'd have to admit she was over thirty-five."
Mary Matthews, 'State of the Union' (1948)

„Eine Frau könnte sich nie um die Präsidentschaft bewerben. Dann müsste sie ja zugeben, dass sie schon über fünfunddreißig ist."
Mary Matthews, *Der beste Mann* (1948)

« Une femme ne pourrait jamais être candidate à la présidence. Elle serait obligée d'admettre qu'elle a plus de trente-cinq ans. »
Mary Matthews, *L'Enjeu* (1948)

ON THE SET OF 'SONG OF LOVE' (1947)
Engaging in physical hijinks with her young, and not-so-young, co-stars. / Leibesertüchtigung mit ihren jungen und nicht mehr ganz so jungen Mitdarstellern. / Acrobaties en compagnie de ses partenaires jeunes et moins jeunes.

PAGES 108/109
STILL FROM 'STATE OF THE UNION' (1948)
Together but apart, as in their off-camera relationship. / Zusammen und doch getrennt – wie auch die Beziehung im wahren Leben. / Ensemble mais séparés, comme dans la vraie vie.

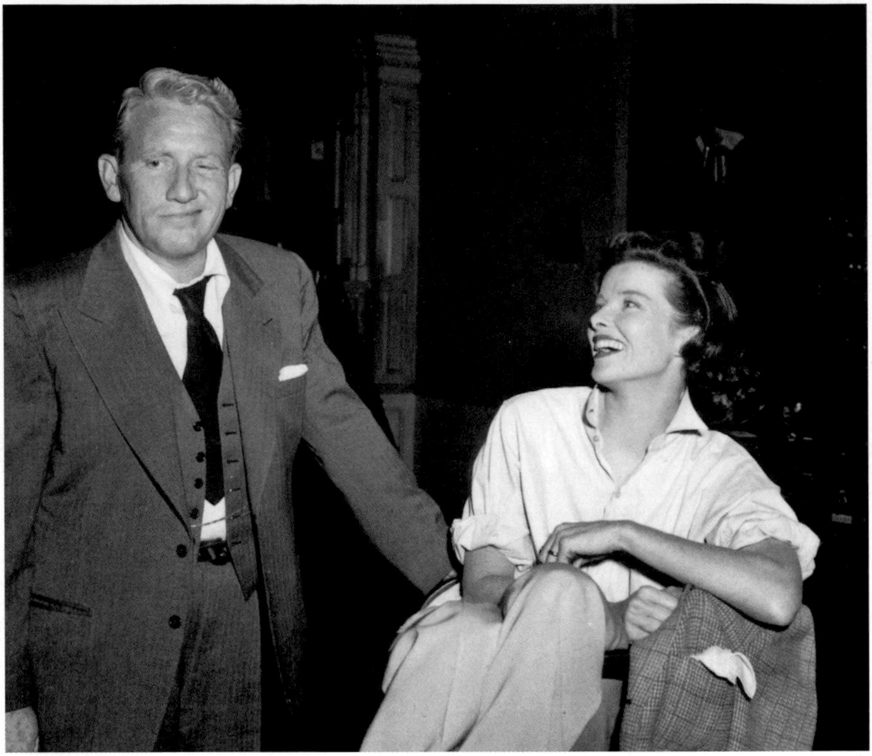

ON THE SET OF 'STATE OF THE UNION' (1948)
A candid moment that captures the two actors at ease with each other. / Der Schnappschuss zeigt die beiden Schauspieler beim ungezwungenen Miteinander. / Moment de détente qui souligne la complicité des deux acteurs.

PAGES 112 & 113
SPENCER TRACY & KATHARINE HEPBURN
The couple rarely appeared in public together and were very discreet about their relationship. / Das Paar zeigte sich selten in der Öffentlichkeit und übte in seiner Beziehung äußerste Diskretion. / Le couple apparaît rarement en public et se montre très discret.

SPENCER TRACY & KATHARINE HEPBURN
Although their relationship lasted almost thirty years, and Tracy was married with children, the studio protected them from scandal. / Obwohl ihre Beziehung fast 30 Jahre lang andauerte und Tracy verheirateter Familienvater war, wurde sie vom Studio gedeckt, um einen Skandal zu verhindern. / Bien que Tracy soit marié et père de famille et que leur liaison dure près de trente ans, les studios évitent le scandale.

STILL FROM 'ADAM'S RIB' (1949)
The Hepburn/Tracy pairing at its peak under Cukor's direction, getting laughs from both tender and tearful moments. / Auf dem Höhepunkt der Zusammenarbeit unter Cukors Regie lacht das Publikum in zärtlichen wie in tränenreichen Szenen über das Paar Hepburn/Tracy. / À son apogée, sous la direction de Cukor, le couple Hepburn/Tracy s'amuse même dans les scènes tendres ou larmoyantes.

STILL FROM 'ADAM'S RIB' (1949)

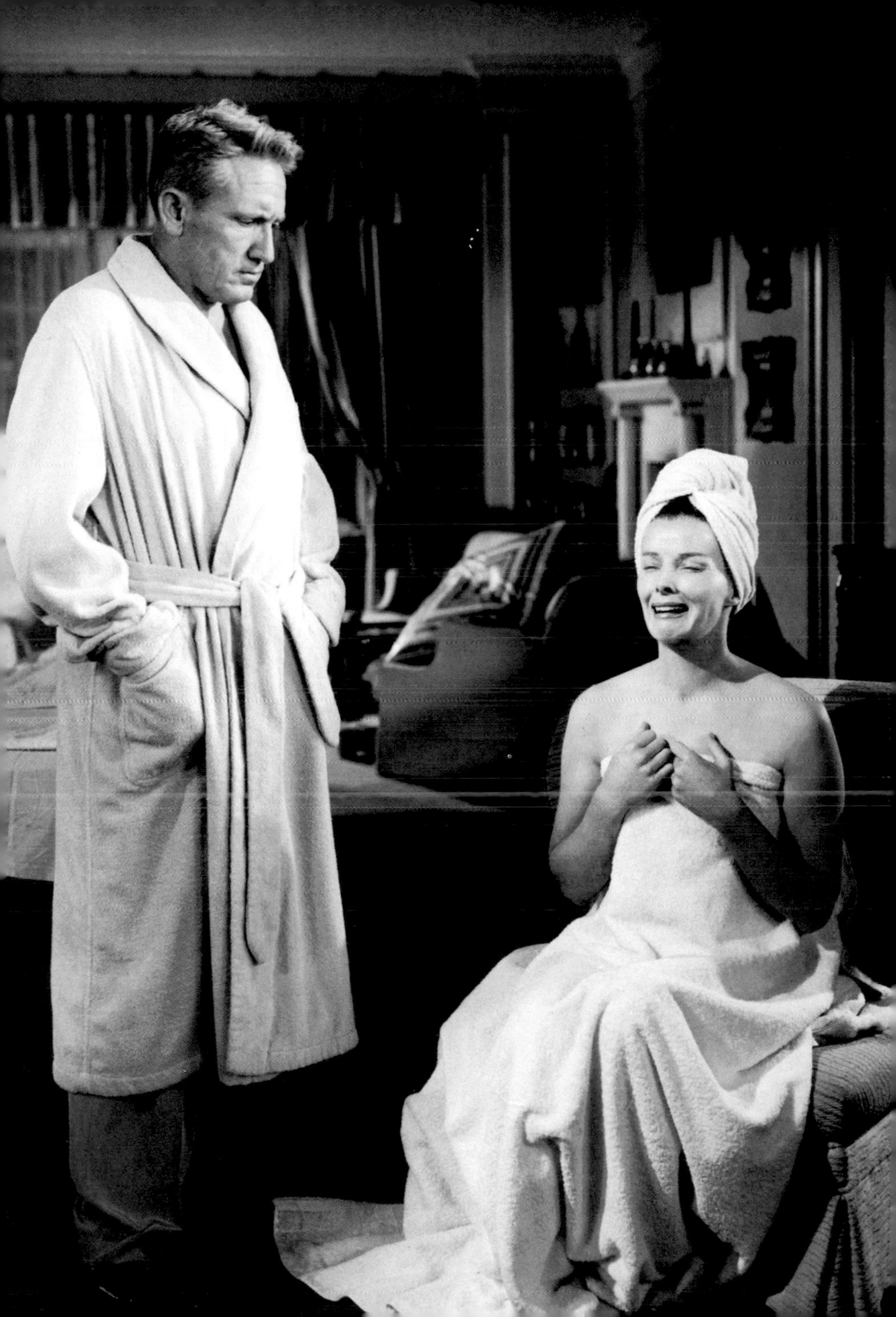

STILL FROM 'ADAM'S RIB' (1949)
Hepburn and Tracy play married lawyers who wage war in the courtroom. / Hepburn und Tracy spielen ein Anwaltsehepaar, das sich im Gerichtssaal bekriegt. / Hepburn et Tracy incarnent un couple d'avocats qui s'affrontent dans le prétoire.

"The ideal American man is certainly Spencer Tracy. And I think I represent a woman. I needle him, and I irritate him, and I try to get around him, and if he put a big paw out and put it on my head, he could squash me. And I think that is the romantic ideal picture of the male and female in this country."
Katharine Hepburn

„Der ideale Amerikaner ist sicherlich Spencer Tracy. Und ich denke, ich stehe für die Frau. Ich ärgere ihn, ich reize ihn, und ich versuche, ihn herumzukriegen, aber wenn er seine große Tatze ausstreckt und sie mir auf den Kopf legt, dann könnte er mich zerquetschen. Und das, denke ich, ist das romantische Idealbild von Mann und Frau in diesem Land."
Katharine Hepburn

STILL FROM 'ADAM'S RIB' (1949)
Judy Holliday is the sometimes bemused defendant. / Judy Holliday wirkt als Angeklagte mitunter leicht verwundert. / Judy Holliday en accusée quelque peu interloquée.

PAGE 118
PORTRAIT FOR 'THE AFRICAN QUEEN' (1951)
An anxious-looking Hepburn would later write about her African experience. / Die hier besorgt dreinblickende Hepburn schrieb später ihre Erinnerungen an die Dreharbeiten in Afrika nieder. / Marquée par son expérience africaine, Hepburn y consacrera plus tard un livre.

« L'Américain idéal est certainement Spencer Tracy. Et je représente une certaine idée de la femme. Je l'asticote, je l'irrite, j'essaie de l'amadouer, et s'il tendait sa grande paluche pour me la flanquer sur la tête, il m'écrabouillerait. Je pense que c'est l'image romantique idéale de l'homme et de la femme dans ce pays. »
Katharine Hepburn

TRANSITION

★

ÜBERGANGSZEIT

LA TRANSITION

STILL FROM 'THE AFRICAN QUEEN' (1951)
Hepburn's experience with Tracy echoed her interaction with Bogart's character. / In Hepburns Verhalten gegenüber der Filmfigur von Bogart spiegelten sich ihre Erfahrungen mit Tracy. / Des échos de sa relation avec Tracy résonnent dans ses rapports avec le personnage de Bogart.

STILL FROM 'THE AFRICAN QUEEN' (1951)
Aboard ship and recalling a similar pose from 'State of the Union.' / Die Einstellung auf dem Boot erinnert an *Der beste Mann*. / Cette nuit à bord du bateau rappelle une scène similaire dans *L'Enjeu*.

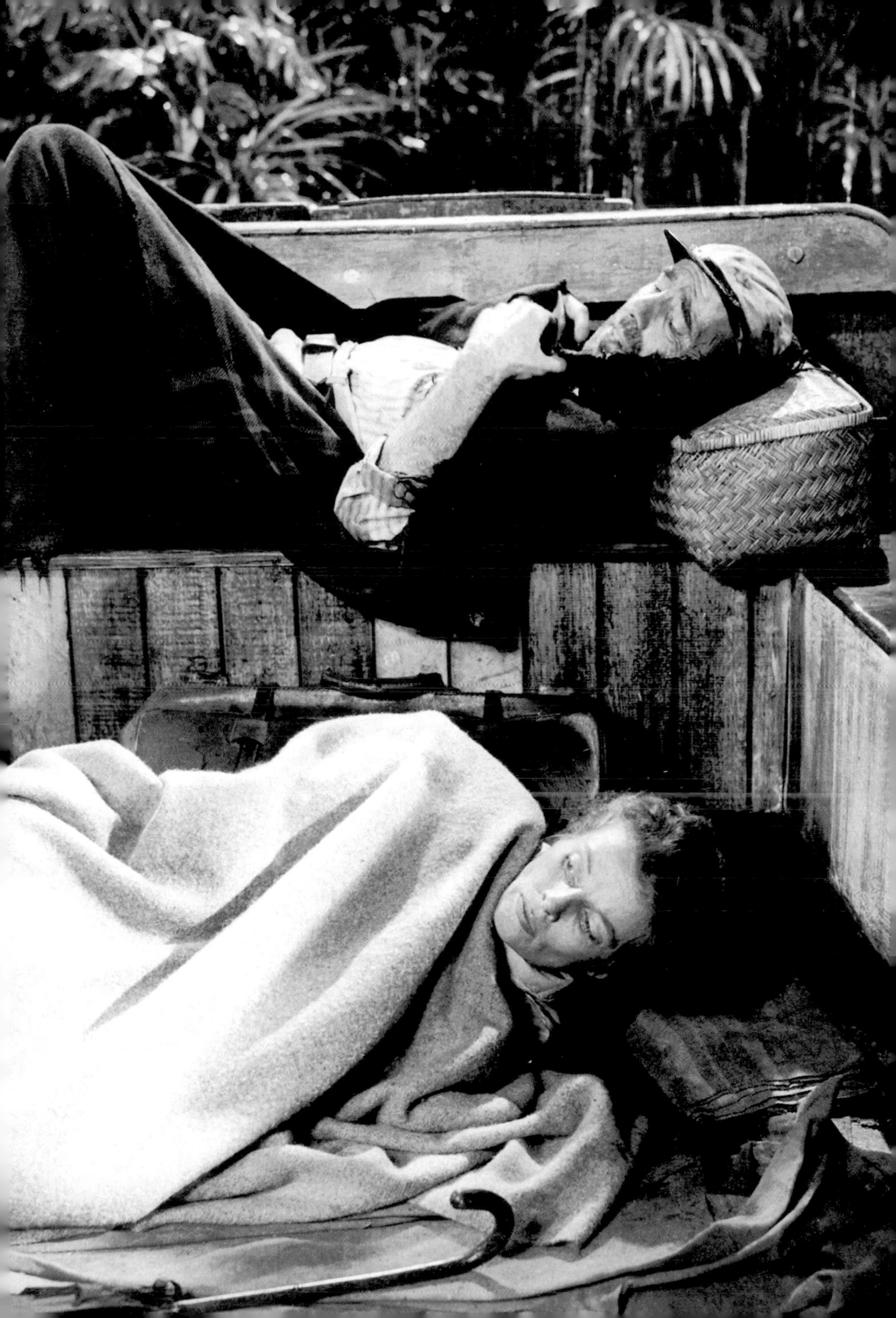

STILL FROM 'THE AFRICAN QUEEN' (1951)
After nearly a decade Hepburn got another Academy Award nomination. / Nach fast einem Jahrzehnt Pause wurde Hepburn wieder für einen Oscar nominiert. / Un rôle qui lui vaut une nouvelle sélection aux Oscars dix ans après la précédente.

ON THE SET OF 'THE AFRICAN QUEEN' (1951)
A familiar characterization, trying to retain one's dignity in adverse conditions. / Eine vertraute Situation: Sie versucht unter widrigen Umständen, Würde zu wahren. / Un personnage familier qui tente de conserver sa dignité face à l'adversité.

STILL FROM 'PAT AND MIKE' (1952)
Tracy and Hepburn's final collaboration with Cukor is arguably their best. / Tracy und Hepburns letzter gemeinsamer Film – *Pat und Mike* – unter der Regie von Cukor gilt allgemein als ihr bester. / La dernière collaboration du couple Tracy/Hepburn avec Cukor dans *Mademoiselle Gagne-tout* est sans doute la meilleure.

"Love has nothing to do with what you are expecting to get, only with what you are expecting to give, which is everything."
Katharine Hepburn

„Liebe hat nichts damit zu tun, was man erwartet zu erhalten, sondern was man vor hat zu geben, nämlich alles."
Katharine Hepburn

« En amour, il ne s'agit pas d'être prêt à recevoir, mais d'être prêt à donner. Tout est là. »
Katharine Hepburn

STILL FROM 'PAT AND MIKE' (1952)
Hepburn easily filled the part of a multi-sport female athlete. / Hepburn fiel die Rolle der vielseitigen Sportlerin leicht, die sich in verschiedenen Disziplinen betätigt. / Hepburn se glisse sans peine dans la peau d'une athlète pluridisciplinaire.

STILL FROM 'SUMMERTIME' (1955)
With Rosanno Brazzi discussing the price of a red vase. / Sie feilscht mit Renato (Rosanno Brazzi) um den Preis einer roten Vase. / L'héroïne discute le prix d'un vase avec Rosanno Brazzi.

STILL FROM 'SUMMERTIME' (1955)
Hepburn was still glamorous as a lonely middle-aged character, feeling that love has passed her by. / Auch als einsame Frau in mittleren Jahren, die meint, die Liebe verpaßt zu haben, konnte Hepburn immer noch glänzen. / Hepburn conserve son éclat dans ce rôle de femme sur le retour qui prend conscience qu'elle est passée à côté de l'amour.

"I said, 'Look, Kate, I'm afraid I can give you no excuse for it, but having done this and that in the middle of the room, you've just got to walk to that window, and I can give you no reason for doing that.' And she said, 'Yeah, well, that's what I'm paid for.' And she did it. And it looked as if the only thing for her to do was to move to that window, so that she could look out. I do admire that professionalism."
David Lean, director

„Ich sagte: ‚Schau mal, Kate, ich fürchte, ich kann es dir nicht erklären, aber nachdem du dies und das mitten im Zimmer getan hast, musst du einfach zum Fenster hinübergehen, und ich kann es nicht weiter begründen.' Und sie sagte: ‚Na gut, dafür werde ich ja bezahlt.' Und sie tat es. Und es wirkte so, als gäbe es nichts anderes, als zum Fenster hinüberzugehen und hinauszuschauen. Diese Professionalität bewundere ich."
David Lean, Regisseur

« J'ai dit : "Écoute, Kate, je ne peux pas te donner de raison valable, mais après avoir fait ceci et cela au milieu de la pièce, il faut que tu marches jusqu'à la fenêtre, ne me demande pas pourquoi." Elle a répondu : "De toutes façons, je suis payée pour ça", et elle s'est exécutée. Et on aurait dit qu'elle ne pouvait faire autrement que d'aller jusqu'à la fenêtre pour regarder dehors. J'admire ce professionnalisme. »
David Lean, cinéaste

PAGES 130/131
STILL FROM 'SUMMERTIME' (1955)
Director David Lean captured the fear and fragility of romance. / Regisseur David Lean fing das Ungewisse und Zerbrechliche der Romanze ein. / Le réalisateur David Lean rend bien la crainte et la fragilité de l'amour.

STILL FROM 'SUMMERTIME' (1955)
Hepburn insisted on falling into the canal; its polluted waters caused an eye infection. / Hepburn bestand darauf, selbst in den Kanal zu fallen, und zog sich in der Kloake eine Augenentzündung zu. / Hepburn insiste pour tomber dans le canal, dont les eaux polluées lui infligeront une infection oculaire.

STILL FROM 'SUMMERTIME' (1955)
It is difficult for Hepburn's character to accept that Brazzi's love is sincere. / Es fällt Jane (Hepburn) schwer zu glauben, dass Renato (Brazzi) seine Liebesschwüre ernst meint. / L'héroïne a peine à croire à la sincérité de son partenaire.

"But she had this thing, this air, you might call it, the most totally magnetic woman I'd ever seen, and probably have ever seen since. She's incredibly down to earth. She can see right through the nonsense in life. She just cares about things that really matter."
Cary Grant, actor

„Aber sie hatte diese Aura ... Wie soll man es ausdrücken? Sie war die anziehendste Frau, die ich bis dahin kennengelernt hatte und wahrscheinlich auch danach. Sie ist unglaublich bodenständig. Sie durchschaut den ganzen Quatsch im Leben. Sie kümmert sich nur um Dinge, die wirklich wichtig sind."
Cary Grant, Schauspieler

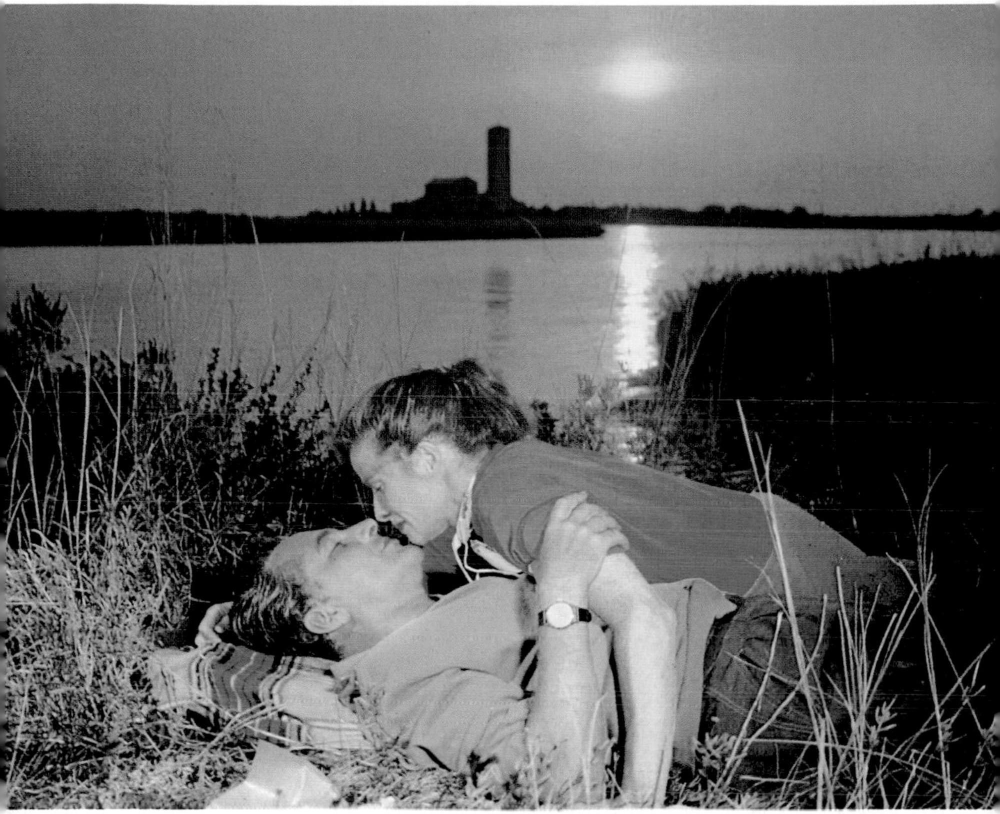

STILL FROM 'SUMMERTIME' (1955)
Hepburn basks in her new-found love. / Jane (Hepburn) genießt ihre neue Liebe. / S'abandonnant enfin au bonheur d'un amour naissant.

« Elle avait quelque chose en elle, c'était la femme la plus charismatique que j'avais jamais vue, et c'est sans doute toujours le cas. Elle a incroyablement les pieds sur terre. Elle perçoit toutes les absurdités de la vie. Elle ne se soucie que de ce qui compte vraiment. »
Cary Grant, acteur

STILL FROM 'THE RAINMAKER' (1956)
Hepburn's third Oscar-nominated spinster takes care of her father and brothers. / Die dritte alte Jungfer, für die Hepburn eine Oscar-Nominierung erhielt, kümmert sich um Vater und Brüder. / Dans son troisième rôle de vieille fille sélectionné aux Oscars, elle veille sur son père et ses frères.

"If you're given a choice between money and sex appeal, take the money. As you get older, the money will become your sex appeal."
Katharine Hepburn

„Wenn du die Wahl hast zwischen Geld und Sex-Appeal, nimm das Geld. Wenn du älter wirst, wird das Geld zu deinem Sex-Appeal."
Katharine Hepburn

« Si vous avez le choix entre l'argent et le sex-appeal, prenez l'argent. Avec l'âge, l'argent vous servira de sex-appeal. »
Katharine Hepburn

STILL FROM 'THE RAINMAKER' (1956)
As in 'Summertime', her character is infatuated with a younger man. / Wie in *Der Traum meines Lebens* verliebt sie sich in einen jüngeren Mann. / Comme dans *Vacances à Venise*, l'héroïne s'éprend d'un homme plus jeune.

STILL FROM 'THE IRON PETTICOAT' (1956)
A uniformed Hepburn was uncomfortable being a 'straight man' for Bob Hope. / Die uniformierte Hepburn fühlte sich unwohl als Stichwortgeberin des Komikers Bob Hope. / Hepburn, en uniforme, n'est guère à l'aise dans le rôle du faire-valoir de Bob Hope.

STILL FROM 'THE IRON PETTICOAT' (1956)
At almost 50 years old, she was equally uncomfortable in lingerie. / Mit fast 50 Jahren fühlte sie sich in Unterwäsche vor der Kamera ebenso unwohl. / À près de 50 ans, elle n'est pas plus à l'aise en dessous sexy.

STILL FROM 'DESK SET' (1957)
This would be Tracy and Hepburn's last 'physical' comedy together. / Dies war die letzte gemeinsame Komödie, in der Tracy und Hepburn Körpereinsatz zeigen mussten. / Ce sera la dernière comédie « physique » que Tracy et Hepburn joueront ensemble.

PAGES 140/141
ON THE SET OF 'SUDDENLY, LAST SUMMER' (1959)
Director Joseph M. Mankiewicz and co-star Montgomery Clift watch Hepburn play a coldly manipulative woman. / Regisseur Joseph M. Mankiewicz und Mitdarsteller Montgomery Clift schauen zu, wie Hepburn eine eiskalte Intrigantin spielt. / Hepburn incarne une femme froide et manipulatrice sous le regard du metteur en scène Joseph M. Mankiewicz et de son partenaire Montgomery Clift.

PORTRAIT FOR 'DESK SET' (1957)
Only seven years Hepburn's senior, an aging Tracy looks much older. / Obwohl Tracy nur sieben Jahre älter war, wirkte er in seinen letzten Lebensjahren deutlich gealtert. / Bien qu'il ne soit que de sept ans son aîné, Spencer Tracy semble beaucoup plus âgé.

STILL FROM 'SUDDENLY, LAST SUMMER' (1959)
Hepburn's understated work earned an eighth Academy Award nomination. / Für ihre zurückhaltende Darstellung wurde Hepburn zum achten Mal für einen Oscar nominiert. / Son jeu tout en retenue lui vaut une huitième sélection aux Oscars.

ON THE SET OF 'SUDDENLY, LAST SUMMER' (1959)
Persistent rumors of discord on the set led to this gag photo proving all the rumours to be true. / Hartnäckige Gerüchte über Dissonanzen bei den Dreharbeiten gaben Anlass zu diesem Juxfoto, dass alle Gerüchte „bestätigte". / Les acteurs s'amusent à corroborer les rumeurs persistantes faisant état de dissensions sur le tournage.

"Say something funny. Make me stop wanting to cry."
Violet Venable, 'Suddenly, Last Summer' (1959)

„Sag was Lustiges. Mach, dass ich nicht mehr weinen will."
Violet Venable, *Suddenly, Last Summer* (1959)

« Dites quelque chose de drôle. Faites que je n'aie plus envie de pleurer. »
Violet Venable, *Soudain l'été dernier* (1959)

STILL FROM 'LONG DAY'S JOURNEY INTO NIGHT' (1962)

As Eugene O'Neill's tortured heroine: another highly acclaimed performance (and Oscar nomination). / Als O'Neills gequälte Heldin: Die vielfach bejubelte Leistung führte zu einer weiteren Oscar-Nominierung. / Hepburn est à nouveau saluée (et sélectionnée aux Oscars) pour son interprétation de l'héroïne torturée d'Eugene O'Neill.

STILL FROM 'LONG DAY'S JOURNEY INTO NIGHT' (1962)

After this incarnation, Hepburn devoted her time to the ailing Tracy's care. / Nach dieser Rolle widmete Hepburn sich der Pflege des kranken Tracy. / Après ce film, elle se consacrera entièrement à Tracy, atteint d'une grave maladie.

PAGE 146

ON THE SET OF 'GUESS WHO'S COMING TO DINNER' (1967)

On or off screen, Hepburn's love for Tracy is obvious. / Auf der Leinwand wie im Leben war Hepburns Liebe zu Tracy offensichtlich. / Son amour pour Tracy transparaît à la ville comme à l'écran.

GRACE

★

ANMUT

LA GRÂCE

ON THE SET OF 'GUESS WHO'S COMING TO DINNER' (1967)
The last hurrah with Spencer Tracy, who died shortly after shooting was completed. / Das letzte Hurra mit Spencer Tracy, der kurz nach Abschluss der Dreharbeiten verstarb. / Son dernier succès avec Spencer Tracy, qui décède peu après la fin du tournage.

"The trouble with Kath is – she understands me."
Spencer Tracy, actor

„Das Problem bei Kath ist – sie versteht mich."
Spencer Tracy, Schauspieler

« Le problème avec Kath, c'est qu'elle me comprend. »
Spencer Tracy, acteur

ON THE SET OF 'GUESS WHO'S COMING TO DINNER' (1967)
Hepburn and Tracy rehearse with their co-stars Sidney Poitier and Katharine Houghton for director Stanley Kramer. / Hepburn und Tracy proben mit ihren Mitdarstellern Sidney Poitier und Katharine Houghton unter der Regie von Stanley Kramer. / Hepburn et Tracy répètent avec leurs partenaires Sidney Poitier et Katharine Houghton, sous la direction de Stanley Kramer.

STILL FROM 'THE LION IN WINTER' (1968)
On location in France for her first picture after Tracy's death. / In Frankreich bei Außenaufnahmen zu ihrem ersten Spielfilm nach Tracys Tod. / Tournage en France pour son premier film après la mort de Tracy.

"I could peel you like a pear, and God himself would call it justice."
Eleanor of Aquitaine, 'The Lion in Winter' (1968)

„Ich könnte Euch wie eine Birne schälen, und Gott selbst nennte es Gerechtigkeit."
Eleanor von Aquitanien, *Der Löwe im Winter* (1968)

« Je pourrais te dépecer comme un lapin et Dieu lui-même n'y verrait que justice. »
Aliénor d'Aquitaine, *Un lion en hiver* (1968)

STILL FROM 'THE LION IN WINTER' (1968)
Another failed romance with a younger man, Peter O'Toole as Henry II. / Eine weitere gescheiterte Romanze mit einem jüngeren Mann: Peter O'Toole als Heinrich II. / Une autre relation ratée avec un homme plus jeune, Peter O'Toole dans le rôle d'Henri II.

PAGES 152/153
STILL FROM 'THE LION IN WINTER' (1968)
An Oscar on merit (after the sentimental award for 'Guess Who's Coming to Dinner'). / Ein wohlverdienter Oscar – nach dem Mitleids-Oscar für *Rat mal, wer zum Essen kommt.* / Un oscar bien mérité après l'oscar « sentimental » reçu pour *Devine qui vient dîner*.

STILL FROM 'THE MADWOMAN OF CHAILLOT' (1969)
Hepburn used costume and bearing to mask her character's eccentricity. / Hinter Kostüm und Gebaren verschleierte Hepburn die Verschrobenheit ihrer Figur. / Ses costumes et son maintien masquent l'excentricité de son personnage.

ON THE SET OF 'THE MADWOMAN OF CHAILLOT' (1969)
With co-performer Danny Kaye. / Mit ihrem Kollegen Danny Kaye. / Avec son partenaire Danny Kaye.

STILL FROM 'THE TROJAN WOMEN' (1971)
Although adhering closely to the text by Euripides, the staging and location work were hard for the almost 65-year-old Hepburn. / Der Film orientierte sich eng am Text von Euripides. Inszenierung und Außenaufnahmen waren dennoch strapaziös für die fast 65-jährige Hepburn. / Bien que le film respecte fidèlement le texte d'Euripide, la mise en scène et le tournage en extérieur sont éprouvants pour l'actrice de près de 65 ans.

ON THE SET OF 'THE TROJAN WOMEN' (1971)

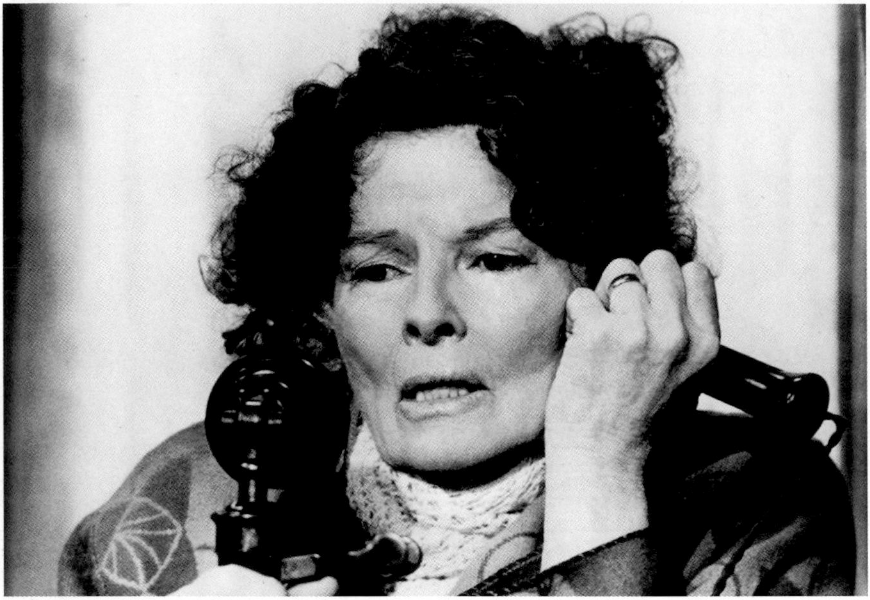

STILL FROM 'THE GLASS MENAGERIE' (1973)
Hepburn's first foray into television drama garnered her first Emmy nomination. / Hepburns erster Ausflug ins Fernsehspiel brachte ihr auch gleich die erste Emmy-Nominierung ein. / Son premier film pour la télévision lui vaut sa première sélection aux Emmy Awards.

"Katharine Hepburn was the template upon which many smart 20th-century women modeled themselves."
Meryl Streep, actress

„Katharine Hepburn war das Muster, an dem sich viele kluge Frauen des 20. Jahrhunderts orientierten."
Meryl Streep, Schauspielerin

« Katharine Hepburn est le modèle dont beaucoup de femmes intelligentes se sont inspirées au XXᵉ siècle. »
Meryl Streep, actrice

STILL FROM 'A DELICATE BALANCE' (1973)
As a Yankee matriarch in another project with autobiographical elements. / Als Matriarchin in Connecticut in einem weiteren Film mit autobiografischen Zügen. / En « matriarche » américaine dans un autre film aux accents autobiographiques.

STILL FROM 'ROOSTER COGBURN' (1975)

"I do not fear a skunk.
I simply do not care for its odor."
Eula Goodnight, 'Rooster Cogburn' (1975)

„Ich habe keine Angst vor Stinktieren.
Ich mache mir nur nichts aus ihrem Geruch."
Eula Goodnight, *Mit Dynamit und frommen Sprüchen* (1975)

« Je n'ai pas peur des putois,
c'est juste que je n'aime pas leur odeur. »
Eula Goodnight, *Une bible et un fusil* (1975)

PORTRAIT FOR 'ROOSTER COGBURN' (1975)
As opposites thrown together, Hepburn and John Wayne revisit the character dynamic and physical action of 'The African Queen.' / Hepburn und John Wayne greifen als gegensätzliche Charaktere, die aufeinander angewiesen sind, auf Figurenkonstellation und Action aus *African Queen* zurück. / Avec leurs caractères opposés, Hepburn et John Wayne revisitent l'action et les relations de *L'Odyssée de l'African Queen*.

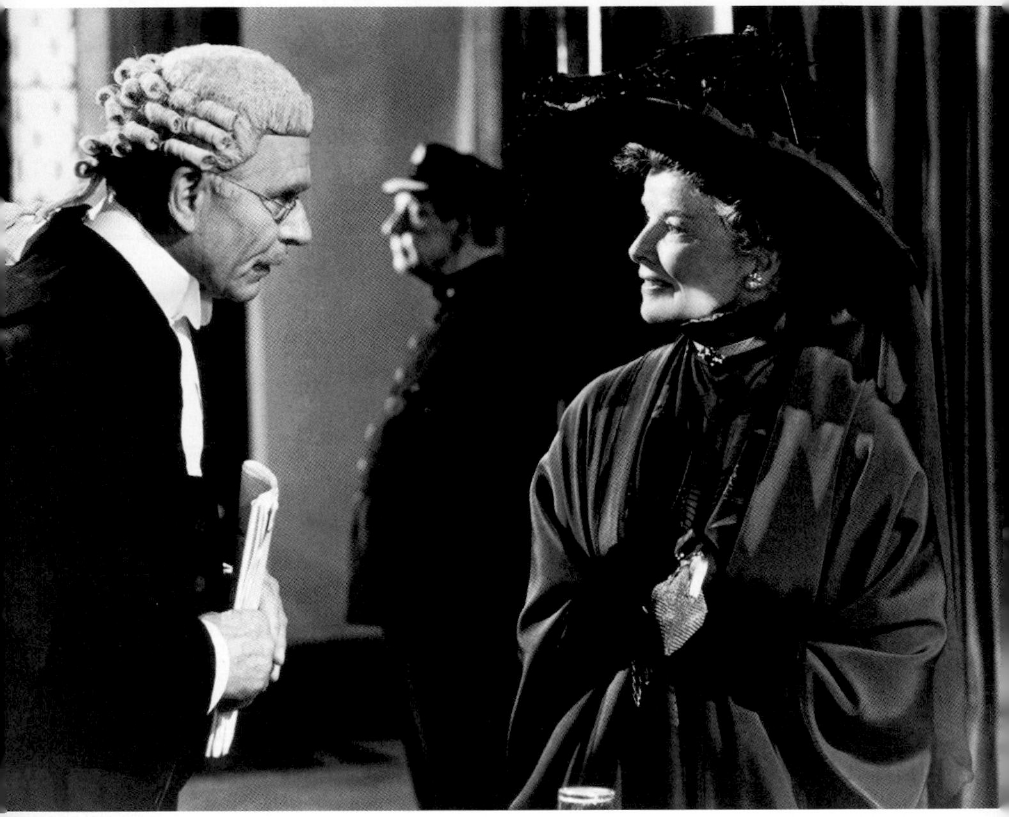

STILL FROM 'LOVE AMONG THE RUINS' (1975)
An aging actress wins an Emmy as an aging actress (opposite Laurence Olivier). / Eine alternde Schauspielerin gewinnt einen Emmy in der Rolle einer alternden Schauspielerin (neben Laurence Olivier). / L'actrice vieillissante remporte un Emmy Award dans le rôle d'une actrice vieillissante (aux côtés de Laurence Olivier).

"Acting's just waiting for the custard pie. That's all."
Katharine Hepburn

„Schauspielen ist nur Warten auf die Sahnetorte. Das ist alles."
Katharine Hepburn

« Jouer la comédie, c'est attendre la tarte à la crème. C'est tout. »
Katharine Hepburn

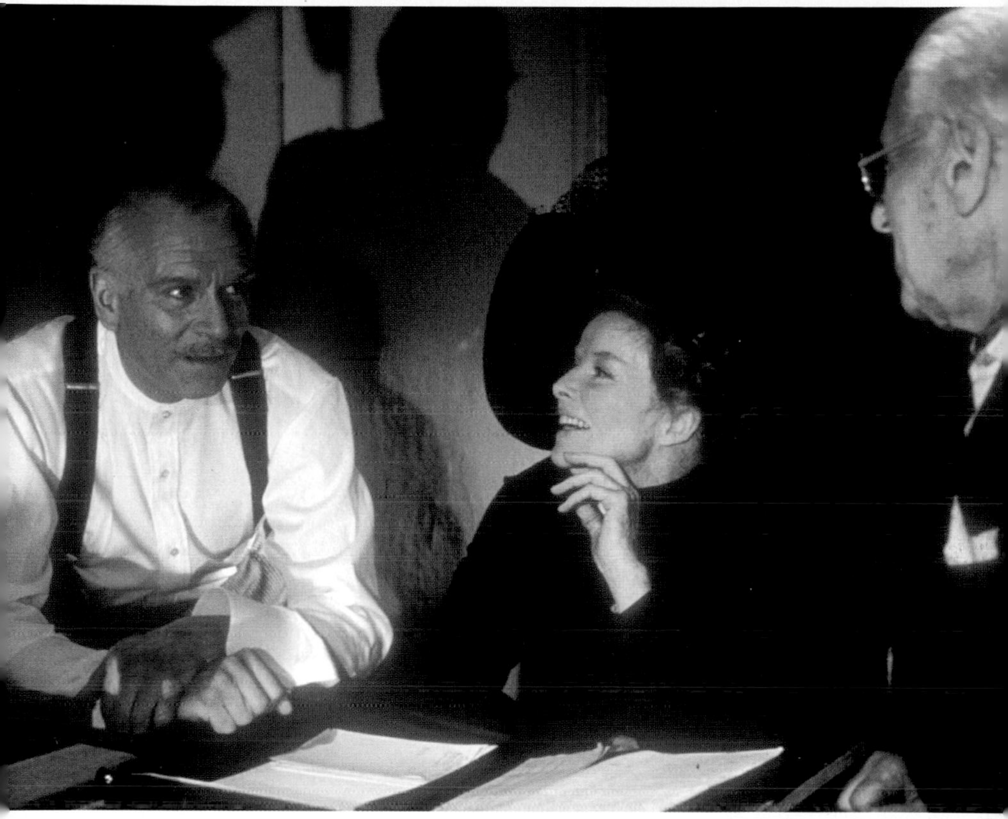

ON THE SET OF 'LOVE AMONG THE RUINS' (1975)

In the 'part' of aging director, her most frequent collaborator George Cukor. / In der „Rolle" des alternden Regisseurs ist George Cukor zu sehen, mit dem sie am häufigsten zusammenarbeitete. / Dans le « rôle » du cinéaste vieillissant, George Cukor, son collaborateur le plus fréquent.

PAGES 164/165

STILL FROM 'THE CORN IS GREEN' (1979)

Carving out a niche in movies-of-the-week and a final project with Cukor. / Im „Fernsehspiel der Woche" hat sie eine Nische für sich entdeckt und dreht einen letzten Film mit Cukor. / Reconvertie dans les téléfilms, elle signe son dernier projet avec Cukor.

STILL FROM 'ON GOLDEN POND' (1981)
Letting Henry Fonda paddle her towards a fourth and final Academy Award. / Henry Fonda paddelt sie hier zu ihrem vierten und letzten Oscar. / Hepburn se laisse guider par Henry Fonda vers son quatrième et dernier oscar.

"I have many regrets and I'm sure everyone does. The stupid things you do, you regret, if you have any sense, and if you don't regret them, maybe you're stupid."
Katharine Hepburn

„Ich bereue viel, und ich bin sicher, es geht jedem so. Wenn man ein wenig Verstand hat, dann bereut man die Dummheiten, die man begangen hat, und wenn man sie nicht bereut, dann ist man vielleicht einfach dumm."
Katharine Hepburn

« J'ai de nombreux regrets, comme tout le monde. Les choses idiotes qu'on a faites, on les regrette si on a un peu de bon sens, et si on ne les regrette pas, c'est qu'on doit être idiot. »
Katharine Hepburn

STILL FROM 'ON GOLDEN POND' (1981)
Hepburn rarely portrayed a wife, a role that also eluded her in life. / Hepburn spielte im Film wie im Leben selten die Ehefrau. / Hepburn joue rarement les épouses, rôle qui lui échappe aussi dans la vie.

ON THE SET OF 'ON GOLDEN POND' (1981)
Rehearsing with director Mark Rydell. / Bei der Probe mit Regisseur Mark Rydell. / Répétition avec le réalisateur Mark Rydell.

"She really is about the only person who gives you the feeling that maybe it could be a woman's world."
Elaine May, actress/writer/director

„Sie ist wirklich so ziemlich die einzige Person, die einem das Gefühl gibt, dies könnte eine Welt für Frauen sein."
Elaine May, Schauspielerin/Schriftstellerin/Regisseurin

« Elle est à peu près la seule personne qui donne l'impression que les femmes pourraient gouverner le monde. »
Elaine May, actrice/scénariste/réalisatrice

PORTRAIT FOR 'ON GOLDEN POND' (1981)
Well past 70, Hepburn again embraced the rigors of location. / Schon weit jenseits der 70 unterwarf sich Hepburn noch einmal den Strapazen von Außenaufnahmen. / À plus de 70 ans, l'actrice affronte encore les rigueurs du tournage en extérieur.

STILL FROM 'THE ULTIMATE SOLUTION OF GRACE QUIGLEY' (1984)
Hepburn's return to features after her near-fatal car accident. / Nach einem beinahe tödlichen Autounfall kehrt Hepburn noch einmal ins Kino zurück. / Hepburn revient au cinéma après l'accident de voiture qui a failli lui être fatal.

PAGES 172/173
STILL FROM 'THE ULTIMATE SOLUTION OF GRACE QUIGLEY' (1984)
Doing her own stunts. / Ihre Stunts spielte sie selbst. / Pas question de se faire doubler dans les scènes d'action.

STILL FROM 'THE ULTIMATE SOLUTION OF GRACE QUIGLEY' (1984)
Again portraying an eccentric but in a very unusual, black comedy. / Wieder spielt sie eine Exzentrikerin, aber diesmal in einer sehr ungewöhnlichen schwarzen Komödie. / Nouveau personnage excentrique dans une comédie noire très originale.

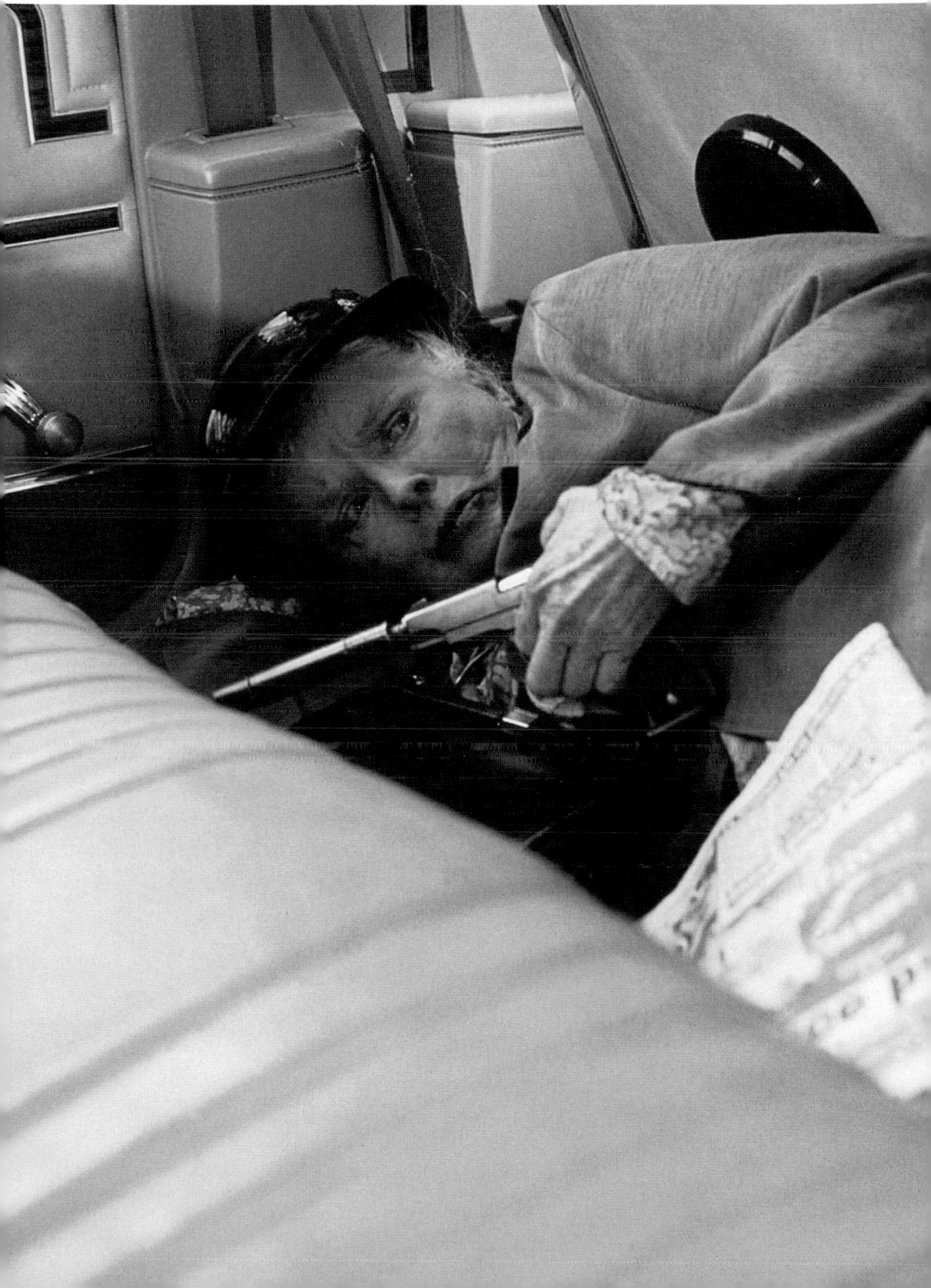

STILL FROM 'TRUMAN CAPOTE'S ONE CHRISTMAS' (1994)

*"If I knew I was going to live to 86
I wouldn't have let the maid go."*
Ginny, 'Love Affair' (1994)

*„Wenn ich gewusst hätte, dass ich mal 86 werde,
hätte ich das Dienstmädchen nie entlassen."*
Ginny, *Perfect Love Affair* (1994)

*« Si j'avais su que je vivrais jusqu'à 86 ans,
je n'aurais pas congédié la bonne. »*
Ginny, *Rendez-vous avec le destin* (1994)

STILL FROM 'MRS. DELAFIELD WANTS TO MARRY' (1986)
Hepburn's effortless television work was consistently award-nominated. / Für ihre mit leichter Hand absolvierten Arbeiten für das Fernsehen wurde Hepburn regelmäßig für Preise nominiert. / Son remarquable travail pour la télévision lui vaut de nombreux prix.

STILL FROM 'LOVE AFFAIR' (1994)
Warren Beatty used all his charm to get Hepburn to take this part and to utter an impolite word on-camera. / Warren Beatty musste all seinen Charme aufbieten, damit Hepburn diese Rolle übernahm und ein äußerst unfeines Wort in die Kamera sprach. / Warren Beatty use de tout son charme pour la convaincre d'accepter ce rôle et de prononcer un gros mot à l'écran.

PAGE 178
COVER OF 'STAGE' (MARCH, 1939)

PORTRAIT FOR 'LOVE AFFAIR' (1994)
Katharine Hepburn's final film appearance. / Katharine Hepburns letzter Filmauftritt. / La dernière apparition de Katharine Hepburn au cinéma.

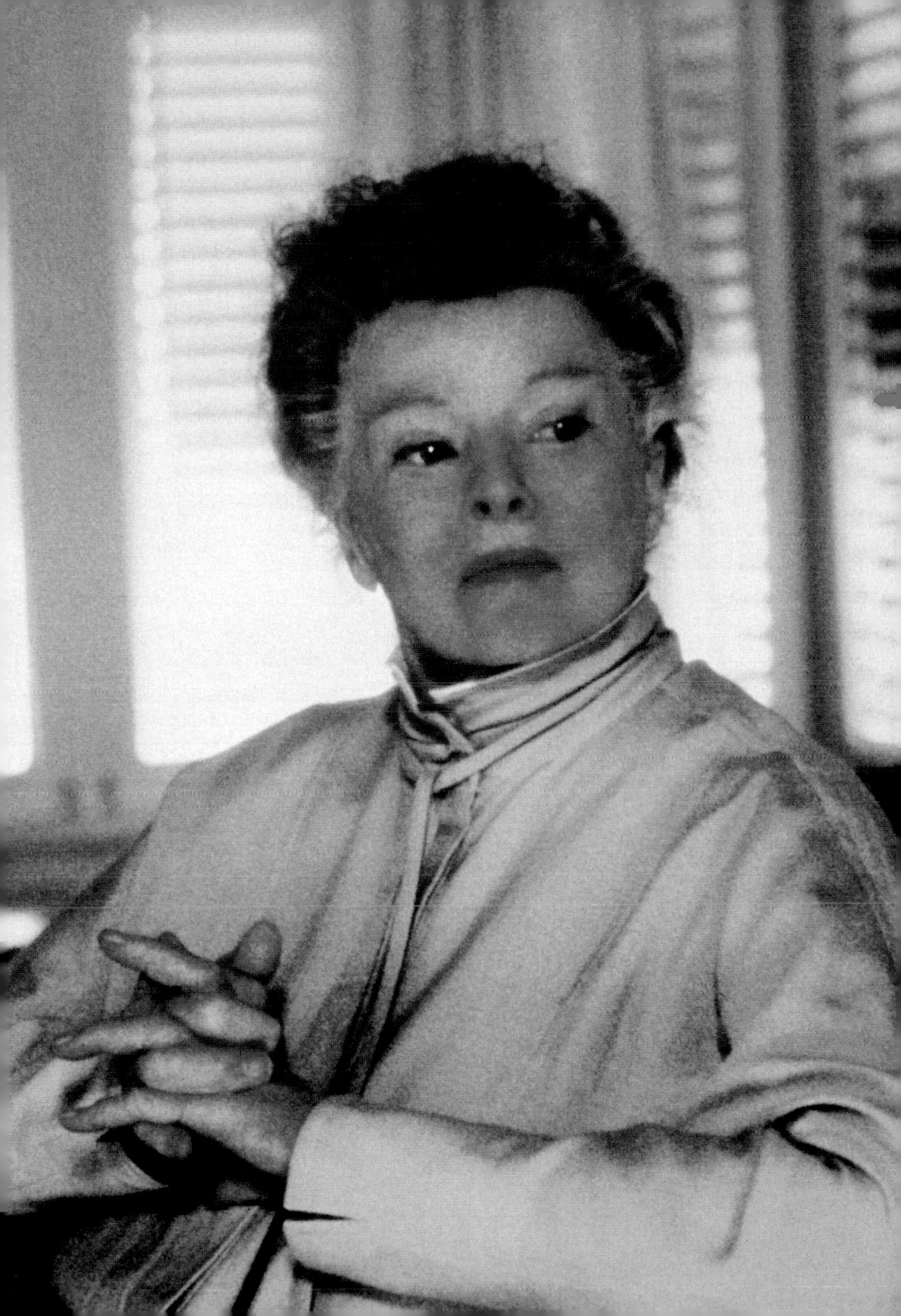

STAGE
THE MAGAZINE OF
After Dark
MARCH 15, 1939
15
Katharine Hepburn
in the
Theatre Guild Production
of Philip Barry's
The Philadelphia Story
VANDAMM

3

CHRONOLOGY

★

CHRONOLOGIE

CHRONOLOGIE

12 May 1907 Katharine Houghton Hepburn is born (second of six children) in Hartford, Connecticut to Katharine Martha Houghton, a suffragette, and Thomas Norval Hepburn, a physician.

1913–1917 During childhood, sometimes shaves her head and calls herself Jimmy.

1921 Discovers the body of her beloved older brother Tom hanging in her aunt's attic. For the next 70 years, takes his birthday as her own.

1928 Graduates from Bryn Mawr College with degrees in history and philosophy. Marries Ludlow Ogden Smith. Stage debut in Baltimore.

1932 After screen test for RKO, receives $1,500 per week to star in *Three Came Unarmed*, which is never made. Film debut opposite John Barrymore in *A Bill of Divorcement*.

1933 *Morning Glory*: First of twelve Academy Award nominations and four awards. Returns to Broadway for *The Lake*, which bombs.

1934 Divorces husband.

1937 Begins two-year relationship with *nouveau riche* Texan Howard Hughes.

1938 Labeled 'box office poison' by Harry Brandt, head of the Independent Theater Owners of America. She buys out her RKO contract.

1940 Makes a package deal with MGM to star in the adaptation of *The Philadelphia Story*, her first hit movie in five years.

1942 Packages and sells *Woman of the Year* to MGM. It is the first of nine movies with Spencer Tracy. This on-and-off-screen relationship continues for 27 years.

1947 Gives speech condemning the House Unamerican Activities Committee for its "smear campaign of the motion picture industry."

1951 *The African Queen* is the first of several transitional roles into portraying middle-aged and often spinsterish women (*Summertime*, *The Rainmaker*, *The Iron Petticoat*, and *Desk Set*).

1962 Begins five years of voluntary retirement to care for an ailing Spencer Tracy.

1967 Agrees to forfeit her salary if Tracy does not complete *Guess Who's Coming to Dinner*. He dies less than a month after completion of filming.

1975 Co-stars with Laurence Olivier in *Love Among the Ruins*, her ninth of ten projects with director George Cukor over a 37-year span.

1979 Screen Actors Guild Life Achievement Award.

1987 Publishes her first book, about the making of *The African Queen*.

1991 Publishes her autobiography.

1999 No. 1 in the American Film Institute survey of Female Screen Legends.

29 June 2003 Dies mid-afternoon in Saybrook. That night theater lights on Broadway are dimmed for a full hour.

COVER OF 'PHOTOPLAY' (APRIL, 1934)

PHOTOPLAY

CENTS
ents in Canada

APRIL

Had To Leave John Gilbert" —Virginia Bruc

Exclusive!
COMPLETE GUIDE TO ANSWERS
IN $250,000 MOVIE QUIZ
Modern Screen
NOVEMBER
10
CENTS
THE LAR
CIRCULAT
OF ANY SC
MAGAZI
WILL AMERICA'S HERO,
HOWARD HUGHES,
Marry
KATHARINE HEPBURN?
Hedy Lamarr's
LIFE STORY!

CHRONOLOGIE

12. Mai 1907 Katharine Houghton Hepburn wird in Hartford, Connecticut, als zweites von sechs Kindern der Suffragette Katharine Martha Houghton und des Arztes Thomas Norval Hepburn geboren.

1913–1917 Während ihrer Kindheit rasiert sie sich gelegentlich den Kopf und nennt sich Jimmy.

1921 Sie entdeckt die Leiche ihres geliebten älteren Bruders Tom, der sich auf dem Dachboden ihrer Tante erhängt hat. Während der nächsten 70 Jahre feiert sie seinen Geburtstag anstelle des eigenen.

1928 Sie verlässt das Bryn-Mawr-College mit einem Abschluss in Geschichte und Philosophie und heiratet Ludlow Ogden Smith. In Baltimore feiert sie ihr Bühnendebüt.

1932 Nach einer Kameraprobe für RKO zahlt man ihr eine Wochengage von $1.500 für eine Hauptrolle in dem Film *Three Came Unarmed*, der nie realisiert wird. Ihr Filmdebüt erlebt sie stattdessen an der Seite von John Barrymore in *A Bill of Divorcement* (*Eine Scheidung*).

1933 *Morning Glory* (*Das neue Gesicht*) bringt die erste von insgesamt zwölf Nominierungen für einen Oscar, den sie viermal gewinnt. Sie kehrt für *The Lake* an den Broadway zurück, doch das Stück floppt.

1934 Sie lässt sich scheiden.

1937 Sie beginnt ein zwei Jahre dauerndes Verhältnis mit dem neureichen Texaner Howard Hughes.

1938 Harry Brandt, der Vorsitzende des Verbands der unabhängigen Kinobesitzer (Independent Theater Owners of America) brandmarkt sie als „Kassengift". Sie kauft sich aus ihrem Vertrag mit RKO heraus.

1940 Sie schließt einen Vertrag mit MGM ab und übernimmt die Hauptrolle in der Verfilmung des Bühnenstücks *The Philadelphia Story* (*Die Nacht vor der Hochzeit*), ihrem ersten Kinoerfolg in fünf Jahren.

1942 Sie schnürt ein Produktionspaket für den Film *Woman of the Year* (*Die Frau, von der man spricht*) und verkauft es an MGM. Es ist der erste von insgesamt neun Filmen mit Spencer Tracy. Die Beziehung zu ihm hat im Film wie im Leben 27 Jahre Bestand.

1947 In einer Rede verurteilt sie den Ausschuss des Repräsentantenhauses zur Untersuchung unamerikanischer Umtriebe (HUAC) scharf wegen seines „Verleumdungsfeldzugs gegen die Filmindustrie".

1951 In *The African Queen* (*African Queen*) spielt sie die erste von mehreren Übergangsrollen als reife, meist altjüngferliche Frau: *Summertime/Summer Madness* (*Der Traum meines Lebens*), *The Rainmaker* (*Der Regenmacher*), *The Iron Petticoat* (*Der eiserne Unterrock*) und *Desk Set* (*Eine Frau, die alles kennt/Eine Frau, die alles weiß*).

1962 Sie zieht sich für fünf Jahre freiwillig vom Film zurück, um den kranken Spencer Tracy zu pflegen.

1967 Sie erklärt sich bereit, auf ihre eigene Gage zu verzichten, falls Tracy den Film *Guess Who's Coming to Dinner* (*Rat mal, wer zum Essen kommt*) nicht fertigstellt. Er stirbt weniger als einen Monat nach Abschluss der Dreharbeiten.

1975 Sie spielt neben Laurence Olivier eine Hauptrolle in dem Fernsehfilm *Love among the Ruins* (*Liebe in der Dämmerung*). Es ist der neunte von insgesamt zehn Filmprojekten unter der Regie von George Cukor in einem Zeitraum von 37 Jahren.

1979 Sie erhält von der Schauspielergewerkschaft (SAG) den „Life Achievement Award" für ihr Lebenswerk.

1987 Ihr erstes Buch erscheint; es handelt von der Entstehung des Films *The African Queen* (*African Queen*).

1991 Ihre Autobiografie erscheint.

1999 In einer Umfrage des amerikanischen Filminstituts (AFI) nach weiblichen Leinwandlegenden belegt sie den ersten Platz.

29. Juni 2003 Sie stirbt am Nachmittag in Saybrook, Connecticut. Am Abend erlöschen alle Lichter am Broadway für eine volle Stunde.

COVER OF 'MODERN SCREEN' (NOVEMBER, 1938)

CHRONOLOGIE

12 mai 1907 Katharine Houghton Hepburn (la deuxième de six enfants) naît à Hartford (Connecticut) d'un mère suffragette, Katharine Martha Houghton, et d'un père chirurgien, Thomas Norval Hepburn.

1913–1917 Durant son enfance, il lui arrive de se raser la tête et de se faire appeler Jimmy.

1921 Découvre le corps de son frère aîné, Tom, pendu dans le grenier de sa tante. Elle considérera désormais l'anniversaire de son frère comme le sien.

1928 Obtient des diplômes d'histoire et de philosophie à l'université de Bryn Mawr. Épouse Ludlow Ogden Smith. Fait ses débuts sur les planches à Baltimore.

1932 Après un bout d'essai pour la RKO, obtient 1 500 dollars par semaine pour jouer dans *Three Came Unarmed*, qui ne sera jamais tourné. Fait ses débuts au cinéma aux côtés de John Barrymore dans *Héritage*.

1933 Reçoit le premier de ses quatre oscars (sur douze sélections) pour *Morning Glory*. Retourne à Broadway pour *The Lake*, qui fait un bide.

1934 Divorce de Ludlow Ogden Smith.

1937 Entame une liaison de deux ans avec le milliardaire Howard Hughes.

1938 Est qualifiée de « poison du box-office » par Harry Brandt, représentant des exploitants de salles indépendants. Rachète son contrat avec la RKO.

1940 Signe un contrat global avec la MGM pour l'adaptation d'*Indiscrétions*, son premier succès en cinq ans.

1942 Vend à la MGM le projet de *La Femme de l'année*. C'est le premier de ses neuf films avec Spencer Tracy. Leur relation à la ville comme à l'écran durera 27 ans.

1947 Prononce un discours condamnant la Commission parlementaire sur les activités anti-américaines pour sa « sa campagne de diffamation contre l'industrie cinématographique ».

1951 Interprète dans *L'Odyssée de l'African Queen* le premier d'une série de rôles de femmes mûres ou de vieilles filles (*Vacances à Venise*, *Le Faiseur de pluie*, *Whisky, vodka et jupon de fer* et *Une femme de tête*).

1962 Interrompt sa carrière pendant cinq ans pour s'occuper de Spencer Tracy, gravement malade.

1967 Accepte de renoncer à son salaire si Tracy ne termine pas *Devine qui vient dîner*. Il décède moins d'un mois après la fin du tournage.

1975 Est la partenaire de Laurence Olivier dans *Il neige au printemps*, le neuvième de ses dix projets (en 37 ans de collaboration) avec le réalisateur George Cukor.

1979 Est récompensée par la Screen Actors Guild pour l'ensemble de sa carrière.

1987 Publie son premier livre, consacré au tournage de *L'Odyssée de l'African Queen*.

1991 Publie son autobiographie.

1999 Classée n° 1 parmi les légendes féminines du cinéma par l'American Film Institute.

29 juin 2003 S'éteint dans l'après-midi à Saybrook. Le soir même, les lumières des théâtres de Broadway sont mises en veilleuse pendant une heure.

COVER OF 'SCREEN BOOK' (JANUARY, 1934)

SCREEN BOOK
MAGAZINE
JAN.
15c in Canada
10 ¢
NRA
KATHARINE HEPBURN
Vill Films
e More Daring In 1934?

R K O RADIO FILMS S.A. Présente
KATHARINE HEPBURN - CARY GRANT
b. lancy
RKO RADIO FILMS
L'IMPOSSIBLE
MONSIEUR BÉBÉ
Mise en scène de HOWARD HAWKS
R. K. O. RADIO FILMS S.A. 52, Champs Elysées . Paris . Bal. 54-55 et la suite

4

FILMOGRAPHY

★

FILMOGRAFIE

FILMOGRAPHIE

FILMS/SPIELFILME/FILMS

A Bill of Divorcement (dt. *Eine Scheidung*, fr. *Héritage*, 1932)
Sydney Fairfield. Director/Regie/réalisation: George Cukor.

Christopher Strong (fr. *Le Phalène d'argent*, 1933)
Lady Cynthia Darrington. Director/Regie/réalisation: Dorothy Arzner.

Morning Glory (dt. *Das neue Gesicht*, fr. *Matin de gloire*, 1933)
Eva Lovelace [Academy Award, Best Actress/Oscar als beste Schauspielerin/oscar de la Meilleure actrice]. Director/Regie/réalisation: Lowell Sherman.

Little Women (dt. *Vier Schwestern*, fr. *Les Quatre Filles du docteur March*, 1933)
Josephine "Jo" March. Director/Regie/réalisation: George Cukor.

Spitfire (fr. *Mademoiselle Hicks*, 1934)
Trigger Hicks. Director/Regie/réalisation: John Cromwell.

The Little Minister (1934)
Barbara, "Lady Babbie". Director/Regie/réalisation: Richard Wallace.

Break of Hearts (fr. *Cœurs brisés*, 1935)
Constance Dane Roberti. Director/Regie/réalisation: Philip Moeller.

Alice Adams (fr. *Désirs secrets*, 1935)
Alice Adams [Academy Award nomination/Oscar-Nominierung/sélection aux Oscars]. Director/Regie/réalisation: George Stevens.

Sylvia Scarlett (1935)
Sylvia Scarlett. Director/Regie/réalisation: George Cukor.

Mary of Scotland (dt. *Maria von Schottland* [aka *Maria Stuart*], fr. *Mary Stuart*, 1936)
Mary Stuart, Queen of Scots/Mary [Maria]Stuart, Königin der Schotten/Mary Stuart, reine d'Écosse. Director/Regie/réalisation: John Ford.

A Woman Rebels (dt. *Ein aufsässiges Mädchen*, fr. *La Rebelle*, 1936)
Pamela Thistlewaite. Director/Regie/réalisation: Mark Sandrich.

Quality Street (fr. *Pour un baiser*, 1937)
Phoebe "Olivia" Throssel. Director/Regie/réalisation: George Stevens.

Stage Door (dt. *Bühneneingang*, fr. *Pension d'artistes*, 1937)
Terry Randall. Director/Regie/réalisation: Gregory La Cava.

Bringing Up Baby (dt. *Leoparden küsst man nicht*, fr. *L'Impossible Monsieur Bébé*, 1938)
Susan Vance. Director/Regie/réalisation: Howard Hawks.

Holiday (dt. *Die Schwester der Braut*, fr. *Vacances*, 1938)
Linda Seton. Director/Regie/réalisation: George Cukor.

The Philadelphia Story (dt. *Die Nacht vor der Hochzeit*, fr. *Indiscrétions*, 1940)
Tracy Samantha Lord [Academy Award nomination/Oscar-Nominierung/sélection aux Oscars]. Director/Regie/réalisation: George Cukor.

Woman of the Year (dt. *Die Frau, von der man spricht*, fr. *La Femme de l'année*, 1942)
Tess Harding [Academy Award nomination/Oscar-Nominierung/sélection aux Oscars]. Director/Regie/réalisation: George Stevens.

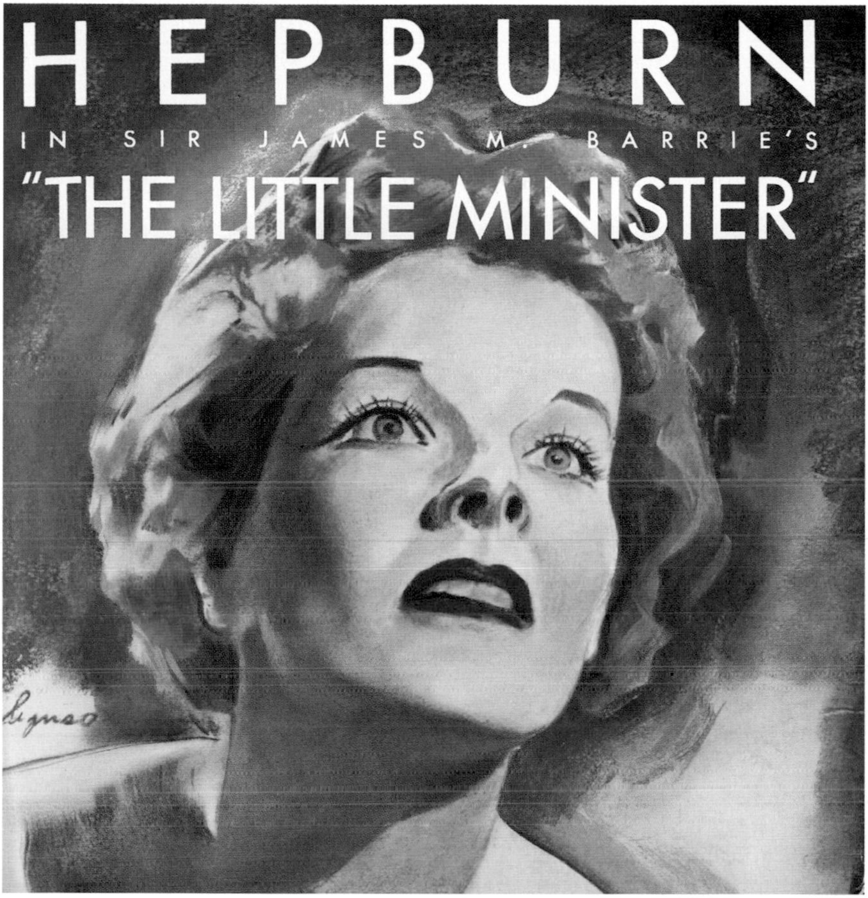

Keeper of the Flame (dt. *Hüter der Flamme* [aka *Die ganze Wahrheit*], fr. *La Flamme sacrée*, 1942)
Christine Forrest. Director/Regie/réalisation: George Cukor.

Stage Door Canteen (fr. *Le Cabaret des étoiles*, 1943)
Herself/als sie selbst/dans son propre rôle. Director/Regie/réalisation: Frank Borzage.

Dragon Seed (dt. *Drachensaat*, fr. *Les Fils du dragon*, 1944)
Jade. Director/Regie/réalisation: Jack Conway & Harold S. Bucquet.

Without Love (dt. *Zu klug für die Liebe*, fr. *Sans amour*, 1945)
Jamie Rowan. Director/Regie/réalisation: Harold S. Bucquet.

Undercurrent (dt. *Die unbekannte Geliebte*, fr. *Lame de fond*, 1946)
Ann Hamilton. Director/Regie/réalisation: Vincente Minnelli.

The Sea of Grass (dt. *Endlos ist die Prärie*, fr. *Le Maître de la prairie*, 1947)
Lutie Cameron Brewton. Director/Regie/réalisation: Elia Kazan.

Song of Love (dt. *Clara Schumanns große Liebe* [aka *Liebesmelodie*], fr. *Passion immortelle*, 1947)

Clara Wieck Schumann. Director/Regie/réalisation: Clarence Brown.

State of the Union (dt. *Der beste Mann*, fr. *L'Enjeu*, 1948)
Mary Matthews. Director/Regie/réalisation: Frank Capra.

Adam's Rib (dt. *Ehekrieg*, fr. *Madame porte la culotte*, 1949)
Amanda Bonner. Director/Regie/réalisation: George Cukor.

The African Queen (dt. *African Queen*, fr. *L'Odyssée de l'African Queen*, 1951)
Rose Sayer [Academy Award nomination/Oscar-Nominierung/sélection aux Oscars]. Director/Regie/réalisation: John Huston.

Pat and Mike (dt. *Pat und Mike*, fr. *Mademoiselle Gagne-tout*, 1952)
Pat Pemberton. Director/Regie/réalisation: George Cukor.

Summertime (aka 'Summer Madness', dt. *Der Traum meines Lebens*, fr. *Vacances à Venise*, 1955)
Jane Hudson [Academy Award nomination/Oscar-Nominierung/sélection aux Oscars]. Director/Regie/réalisation: David Lean.

The Rainmaker (dt. *Der Regenmacher*, fr. *Le Faiseur de pluie*, 1956)
Lizzie Curry [Academy Award nomination/Oscar-Nominierung/sélection aux Oscars]. Director/Regie/réalisation: Joseph Anthony.

The Iron Petticoat (dt. *Der eiserne Unterrock*, fr. *Whisky, vodka et jupon de fer*, 1956)

Vinka Kovelenko. Director/Regie/réalisation: Ralph Thomas.

Desk Set (dt. *Eine Frau, die alles kennt* [aka *Eine Frau, die alles weiß*], fr. *Une femme de tête*, 1957)
Bunny Watson. Director/Regie/réalisation: Walter Lang.

Suddenly, Last Summer (dt. *Plötzlich im letzten Sommer*, fr. *Soudain l'été dernier*, 1959)
Violet Venable [Academy Award nomination/Oscar-Nominierung/sélection aux Oscars]. Director/Regie/réalisation: Joseph L. Mankiewicz.

Long Day's Journey Into Night (fr. *Long voyage dans la nuit*, 1962)
Mary Tyrone [Academy Award nomination/Oscar-Nominierung/sélection aux Oscars]. Director/Regie/réalisation: Sidney Lumet.

Guess Who's Coming to Dinner (dt. *Rat mal, wer zum Essen kommt*, fr. *Devine qui vient dîner...*, 1967)
Christina Drayton [Academy Award, Best Actress/Oscar als beste Schauspielerin/oscar de la Meilleure actrice]. Director/Regie/réalisation: Stanley Kramer.

The Lion in Winter (dt. *Der Löwe im Winter*, fr. *Un lion en hiver*, 1968)

Eleanor of Aquitaine [Academy Award, Best Actress]/Eleanor von Aquitanien [Oscar als beste Schauspielerin]/Aliénor d'Aquitaine [oscar de la Meilleure actrice]. Director/Regie/réalisation: Anthony Harvey.

The Madwoman of Chaillot (dt. *Die Irre von Chaillot*, fr. *La Folle de Chaillot*, 1969)
Countess Aurelia/Gräfin Aurelia/Comtesse Aurelia. Director/Regie/réalisation: Bryan Forbes.

The Trojan Women (dt. *Die Trojanerinnen*, fr. *Les Troyennes*, 1971)
Hecuba/Hécube. Director/Regie/réalisation: Michael Cacoyannis.

A Delicate Balance (dt. *Empfindliches Gleichgewicht*, 1973)
Agnes. Director/Regie/réalisation: Tony Richardson.

Rooster Cogburn (dt. *Mit Dynamit und frommen Sprüchen*, fr. *Une bible et un fusil*, 1975)
Eula Goodnight. Director/Regie/réalisation: Stuart Millar.

Olly, Olly, Oxen Free (dt. *Das große Abenteuer im Ballon*, 1978)
Miss Pudd. Director/Regie/réalisation: Richard A. Colla.

On Golden Pond (dt. *Am goldenen See*, fr. *La Maison du lac*, 1981)
Ethel Thayer [Academy Award, Best Actress/Oscar als beste Schauspielerin/oscar de la Meilleure actrice]. Director/Regie/réalisation: Mark Rydell.

The Ultimate Solution of Grace Quigley (dt. *Grace Quigleys letzte Chance*, fr. *Grace Quigley*, 1984)
Grace Quigley. Director/Regie/réalisation: Anthony Harvey.

Love Affair (dt. *Perfect Love Affair*, fr. *Rendez-vous avec le destin*, 1994)
Ginny. Director/Regie/réalisation: Glenn Gordon Caron.

TELEVISION FILMS/FERNSEHSPIELE/ TÉLÉVISION

The Glass Menagerie (1973)
Amanda Wingfield [Emmy Award nomination/Emmy-Nominierung/sélection aux Emmy Awards]. Director/Regie/réalisation: Anthony Harvey.

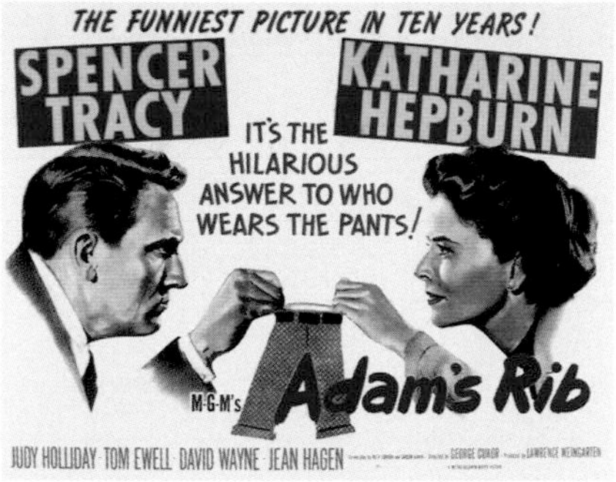

Love Among the Ruins (dt. *Liebe in der Dämmerung*, fr. *Il neige au printemps*, 1975)
Jessica Medlicott [Emmy Award, Outstanding Actress/Emmy als herausragende Schauspielerin/Emmy Award de la Meilleure actrice]. Director/Regie/réalisation: George Cukor.

The Corn is Green (dt. *Das Korn ist grün*, fr. *Le Blé est vert*, 1979)
Miss Lilly C. Moffat [Emmy Award nomination/Emmy-Nominierung/sélection aux Emmy Awards]. Director/Regie/réalisation: George Cukor.

Mrs. Delafield Wants to Marry (dt. *Mrs. Delafield will heiraten*, fr. *Mariage interdit*, 1986)
Margaret Delafield [Emmy Award nomination/Emmy-Nominierung/sélection aux Emmy Awards]. Director/Regie/réalisation: George Shaefer.

Laura Lansing Slept Here (dt. *Eine Dame namens Laura*, fr. *La Folle Semaine de Laura Lansing*, 1988)
Laura Lansing. Director/Regie/réalisation: George Shaefer.

The Man Upstairs (dt. *Kein Engel auf Erden*, 1992)
Victoria Brown. Director/Regie/réalisation: George Shaefer.

This Can't be Love (dt. *Liebe ist nicht bloß ein Wort*, fr. *Est-ce bien de l'amour ?*, 1994)
Marion Bennett. Director/Regie/réalisation: Anthony Harvey.

Truman Capote's One Christmas (dt. *Eine Weihnacht*, 1994)
Cornelia Beaumont. Director/Regie/réalisation: Tony Bill.

BIBLIOGRAPHY

WRITTEN BY KATHARINE HEPBURN/BÜCHER VON KATHARINE HEPBURN/LIVRES DE KATHARINE HEPBURN

'Lauren Bacall' in **Roddy McDowell:** *Double Exposure*. Delacorte, 1966.

The Making of the African Queen Or: How I Went to Africa With Bogart, Bacall and Huston and Almost Lost My Mind. Knopf, 1987.

Me: Stories of My Life. Knopf, 1991.

Katharine Hepburn's World of Stories. Interlink, 1999.

BOOKS/BÜCHER/LIVRES

Andersen, Christopher: *An Affair to Remember: The Remarkable Love Story of Katharine Hepburn and Spencer Tracy*. Avon, 1998.

Andersen, Christopher: *Young Kate*. Delta, 1990.

Berg, A. Scott: *Kate Remembered*. Putnam, 2003.

Bergan, Ronald: *Katharine Hepburn: An Independent Woman*. Arcade, 1996.

Britton, Andrew: *Katharine Hepburn: Star as Feminist*. Columbia University Press, 2003.

Bryson, John: *The Private World of Katharine Hepburn*. Little, Brown, 1992.

Carey, Gary: *Katharine Hepburn: Hollywood Yankee*. Thorndike, 1984.

Carr, Larry: *More Fabulous Faces: The Evolution and Metamorphosis of Dolores Del Rio, Myrna Loy, Carole Lombard, Bette Davis, and Katharine Hepburn*. Doubleday, 1979.

Crimp, Susan: *Katharine Hepburn Once Said...: Great Lines to Live By*. Harper, 2003.

Danielson, Sarah Parker: *Katharine Hepburn: A Hollywood Portrait*. Smithmark, 1993.

Dickens, Homer & Quick, Laurence J.: *The Films of Katharine Hepburn*. Carol, 1990.

Edwards, Anne: *Katharine Hepburn: A Remarkable Woman*. William Morrow, 1989.

Freedland, Michael: *Katharine Hepburn*. W. H. Allen, 1984.

Harvey, Diana Karanikas & Harvey, Jackson: *Katharine Hepburn: A Life in Pictures*. Friedman Fairfax, 1998.

Higham, Charles: *Kate: The Life of Katharine Hepburn*. W. W. Norton, 2004.

Hodge, Jessica: *Hollywood Legends: Katharine Hepburn*. Crescent, 1992.

Holland, Barbara: *Katharine Hepburn*. Random House, 1998.

Johnson, Marilyn: *Katharine Hepburn: 1907–2003*. Life Books, 2003.

Kanin, Garson: *Tracy and Hepburn*. Viking, 1971.

Latham, Caroline: *Katharine Hepburn: Her Film and Stage Career*. Proteus, 1985.

Leaming, Barbara: *Katharine Hepburn*. Limelight, 2004.

Marill, Alvin H.: *Katharine Hepburn*. Pyramid, 1973.

Morley, Sheridan: *Katharine Hepburn: A Celebration*. Michael Joseph, 1984.

Parish, James Robert: *Katharine Hepburn: The Untold Story*. Alyson, 2005.

Porter, Darwin: *Katharine the Great: A Lifetime of Secrets Revealed (1907-1950)*. Blood Moon, 2004.

Prideaux, James: *Knowing Hepburn and Other Curious Experiences*. Faber & Faber, 1996.

Ryan, Joal: *Katharine Hepburn: A Stylish Life*. St. Martin's, 1999.

Smith, Warren Allen: *Celebrities in Hell*. Barricade, 2002.

Spada, James: *Hepburn, Her Life in Pictures*. Doubleday, 1984.

Tarshis, Lauren: *Kate: The Katharine Hepburn Album*. Perigee, 1993.

Thain, Andrea: *Katharine Hepburn. Eine Biographie*. Rowohlt, 1993.

Waterman, Ivan: *Katharine Hepburn*. Haus, 2006.

IMPRINT

Hohenzollernring 53, D-50672 Köln
www.taschen.com

This 2008 edition published by Barnes & Noble, Inc., by arrangement with TASCHEN GmbH.

Editor/Picture Research/Layout: Paul Duncan/Wordsmith Solutions
Editorial Coordination: Martin Holz, Cologne
Production Coordination: Nadia Najm and Horst Neuzner, Cologne
German Translation: Thomas J. Kinne, Nauheim
French Translation: Anne Le Bot, Paris
Multilingual Production: www.arnaudbriand.com, Paris
Typeface Design: Sense/Net, Andy Disl and Birgit Reber, Cologne

Barnes & Noble, Inc.
122 Fifth Avenue
New York, NY 10011

ISBN-13: 978-1-4351-0715-1
ISBN-10: 1-4351-0715-2

Printed in China

10 9 8 7 6 5 4 3 2 1

All the photos in this book, except for those listed below, were supplied by The Kobal Collection.
The Jim Heimann Collection: p. 181, 185

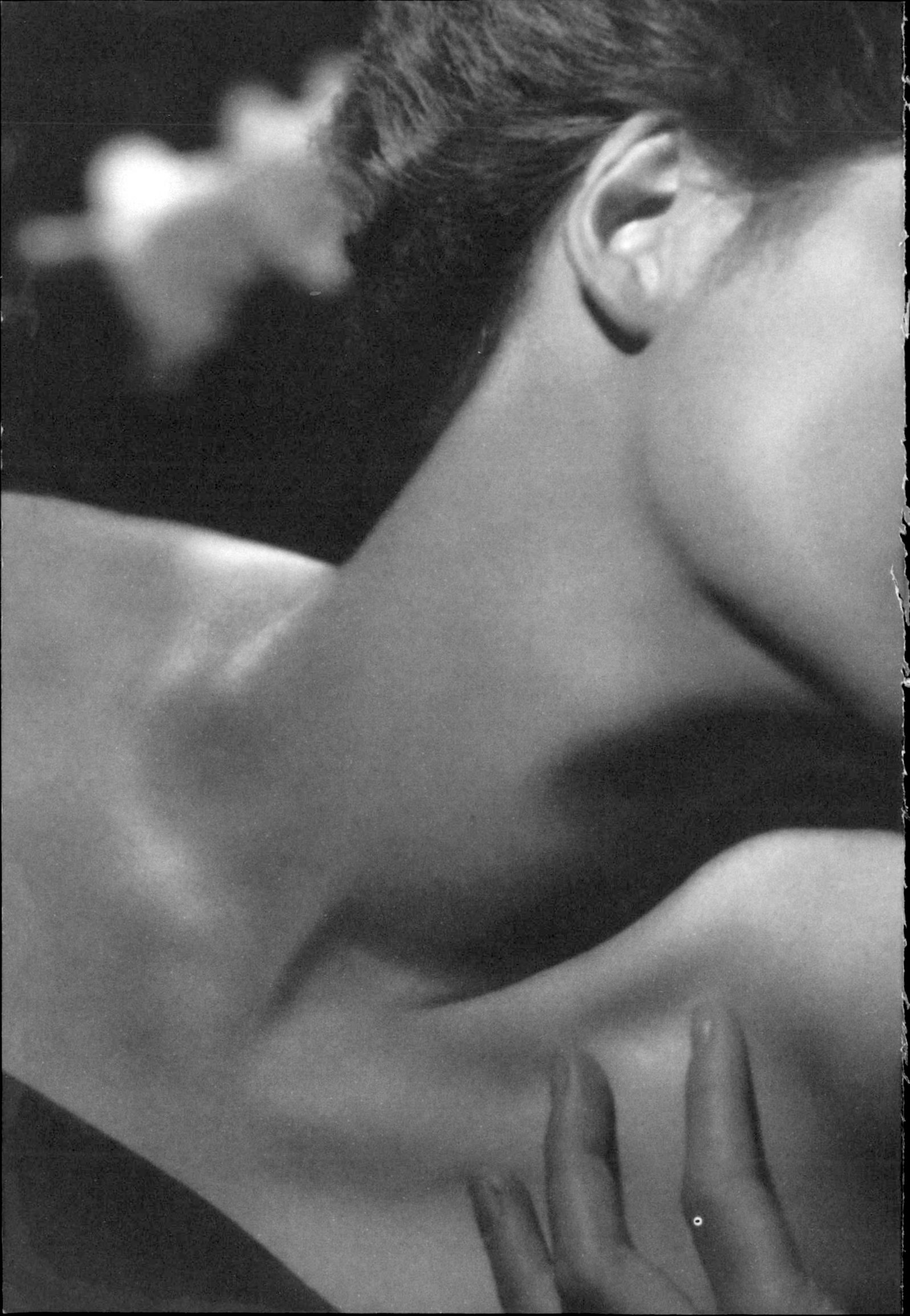